AS/A-LEVEL YEAR 1

STUDENT GUIDE

EDEXCEL

Business

Theme 1

Marketing and people

Mark Hage

Series editor: Ian Marcousé

HODDER
EDUCATION
AN HACHETTE UK COMPANY

Hodder Education, an Hachette UK company, Blenheim Court, George Street, Banbury, Oxfordshire OX16 5BH

Orders

Bookpoint Ltd, 130 Park Drive, Milton Park, Abingdon, Oxfordshire OX14 4SB

tel: 01235 827827

fax: 01235 400401

e-mail: education@bookpoint.co.uk

Lines are open 9.00 a.m.–5.00 p.m., Monday to Saturday, with a 24-hour message answering service. You can also order through the Hodder Education website: www.hoddereducation.co.uk

ISBN 978-1-4718-8316-3

First printed 2017

Impression number 5 4 3 2

Year 2021 2020 2019 2018 2017

This Guide has been written specifically to support students preparing for the Edexcel AS and A-level Business examinations. The content has been neither approved nor endorsed by Edexcel and remains the sole responsibility of the author.

Typeset by Integra Software Services Pvt. Ltd., Pondicherry, India

Cover photo anake/Fotolia

Printed in Dubai

Hachette UK's policy is to use papers that are natural, renewable and recyclable products and made from wood grown in sustainable forests. The logging and manufacturing processes are expected to conform to the environmental regulations of the country of origin.

Contents

Content Guidance

Questions & Answers

■Getting the most from this book

Exam tips

Advice on key points in the text to help you learn and recall content, avoid pitfalls, and polish your exam technique in order to boost your grade.

Knowledge check

Rapid-fire questions throughout the Content Guidance section to check your understanding.

Knowledge check answers

1 Turn to the back of the book for the Knowledge check answers.

Summaries

■ Each core topic is rounded off by a bullet-list summary for quick-check reference of what you need to know.

Exam-style questions

Commentary on the questions

Tips on what you need to do to gain full marks, indicated by the icon 🅮

Sample student answers

Practise the questions, then look at the student answers that follow.

Commentary on sample student answers

Read the comments (preceded by the icon 🅮) showing how many marks each answer would be awarded in the exam and exactly where marks are gained or lost.

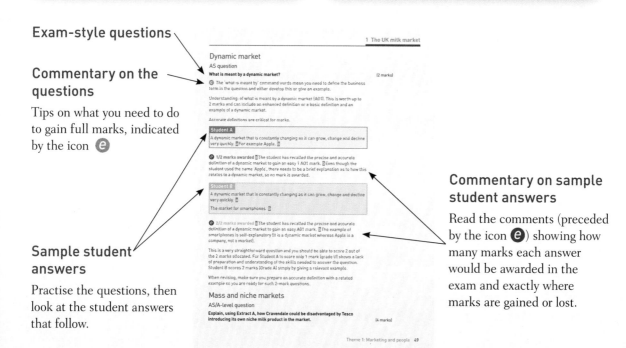

■About this book

This guide (Student Guide 1) and its companions (Student Guides 2, 3, 4) have been written with one thing in mind: to provide you with the ideal resource for your revision of both the Edexcel Business AS and the first year of the Edexcel Business A-level.

In your study of the subject you will look at business in a variety of contexts, small and large, national and global, service and manufacturing. The themes of the AS Business specification are marketing and managing business decisions. The themes of A-level Business also include business decisions and strategy and global business.The focus of Student Guide 1 is the following:

- Meeting customer needs – meeting customers' needs, market research and market positioning.
- The market – demand, supply, elasticity of demand, elasticity of supply.
- Marketing mix and strategy – the marketing mix, product design, branding and promotion, pricing strategies, distribution, marketing strategy.
- Managing people – approaches to staffing, recruitment, selection and training, organisational design, motivational theory and practice.
- Entrepreneurs and leaders – leadership, role of the entrepreneur, entrepreneurial motives and characteristics, business objectives, forms of business, business choices, moving from entrepreneur to leader.

Content Guidance

The Content Guidance section offers concise coverage combining an overview of key terms and concepts with identification of opportunities for you to illustrate higher-level skills of analysis and evaluation.

The specifications assume students have no pre-existing experience of the subject and its key terms. The most important factor at this stage is an interest in business in the news. Business is a subject that requires you to apply key terms to real businesses, so an interest in businesses such as Apple and McDonald's will help you to contextualise the theories covered. This is the most enjoyable part of the subject and allows you to score highly in the exam.

Questions & Answers

The Questions & Answers section provides three examples of stimulus materials with the various types of questions that you are likely to be faced with: short answer, data response and open response questions. The questions cover both AS and A-level Business, and are annotated to show which course they are relevant to. They also give explanations of command words which can be applied to any question with the same word. The answers are also explained in detail, including the grades obtained.

A common problem for students and teachers is the lack of resources, and in particular exam-style questions that cover individual areas of study. The questions in this guide are tailored so you can apply your learning while the topic is still fresh in your mind, either during the course itself or when you have revised a topic in preparation for the examination. Along with the sample answers this should provide you with a sound basis for sitting your exams in Business.

Content Guidance

■ Meeting customer needs

The market

Mass markets

Mass market refers to a large market of customers with widely different backgrounds that a business will not try to distinguish between, said to be **undifferentiated**.

An example of a mass market is the selling of milk in supermarkets. Milk is sold in many different shops, with the product varying little in quality or looks, therefore being undifferentiated.

Advantages of operating in a mass market include being able to purchase goods and materials in bulk, known as **economies of scale**, and dealing with high sales volumes, which make it easier to afford large advertising and marketing campaigns.

The disadvantage to being in a mass market is that the competition is likely to be fierce as businesses are attracted to potentially high sales levels. To stand out from the crowd, a **unique selling point** is hugely helpful – for example, Bounty, the only chocolate bar filled with coconut.

> **Exam tip**
> You will gain the most marks by relating your analysis of mass markets to the stimulus material.

Mass market
A large market of customers which is undifferentiated and that sells products and services to suit a large number of consumers.

Knowledge check 1

Name two features of a mass market.

Niche markets

A niche market is the smaller section of a larger market on which a product or service is focused. Businesses operating in a niche market aim to satisfy specific market needs by creating a carefully tailored product.

An example of a niche market would be specialised milk such as filtered milk, which is a smaller section of the milk market. Not all shops sell filtered milk, so it is uncommon in terms of its availability. In addition, it is aimed at meeting different customer needs, of those customers who want a product that is perceived as being of a higher quality than ordinary milk.

The advantages of a business being in a niche market are there is less competition from other businesses and products can be tailored to meet customers' needs.

The disadvantage of a business being in a niche market is that, as this is a smaller part of the larger market, there are fewer potential customers, therefore it may be difficult to persuade retailers to stock the product(s).

Niche market A smaller part of a large market, with products tailored to specific customer needs.

Knowledge check 2

Lindor chocolate was once in a tiny, luxury niche; now it's a mass market brand. What benefits may brand owner Lindt gain from this?

Differences between niche and mass markets

A niche market is small but focused on one specific type of customer. A mass market product may have a lower price than a niche market product.

Identifying a new niche market is a classic way in which new small firms can find a profitable niche for themselves.

Dynamic markets

A **dynamic market** emerges, grows, changes and can decline very quickly. If a market is changing constantly, it is likely to be a dynamic market. Examples include technology markets, such as social media or e-commerce.

A dynamic market can make it difficult for a business to forecast sales of its products due to rapid change and/or rapid growth. For example, customer **demand** is likely to be unpredictable in a dynamic market as customers' wants and needs evolve more quickly.

The effect of competition on price and demand

Competition is where rival businesses in the same market try to win customers from each other. Businesses can gain customers through using the **price** of their product or service, for example by offering a lower price for a product or service that is similar to that of a competing business.

The difference between risks and uncertainty

Risks in business are factors that are not expected but can be quantified, such as the risk of your factory being flooded (in London, close to zero, thanks to the Thames Barrier; in Keswick, Cumbria, as high as 1 in 10 each year).

Uncertainty is being unsure of the factors influencing sales and therefore being unable to predict what will happen to the business in terms of its profits or growth. A business might try to minimise uncertainty by using market research to anticipate the likely effect its decisions will have on its position in the market.

Market research

Market research involves gathering information about customers' attitudes, behaviour and wants in relation to a product or service.

Businesses often complete market research before entering a new market and at various times while operating in a market. For example, market research can check whether customer loyalty is being maintained or is starting to slip – and how best to tackle any slippage, for instance allowing customers to identify improvements in the service in a survey.

Product orientation

Product orientation is where a business focuses primarily on creating and developing a high-quality good or service – but perhaps ignoring customer preferences and priorities.

The advantage of a business being product orientated is that it allows the business to focus on product quality and innovation and spend most of its efforts and money on doing this. Toyota is noted for this – and which is the world car market's top-selling company? Toyota.

Dynamic market A market that is constantly changing – it can grow, change and decline very quickly.

Demand The amount of a good or service which a consumer buys at a given price.

Price The value at which a product or service is offered to customers.

Knowledge check 3

Name one effect price has on demand.

Market research Information is gathered on customers – their attitudes, behaviour and wants – in relation to a product or service.

The disadvantages are that focusing on the product and putting customer priorities in second place may mean the product is admired but does not sell well. Nokia was convinced its smartphones were better than Apple's. Customers disagreed.

Market orientation

Market orientation is where a business chooses to design a product or service to meet the requirements of customer preferences/desires. Market research is critical to the success of a market-orientated business as it allows the business to find out customers' tastes and priorities.

The advantages of a business being market orientated are the close fit with customer expectations and greater responsiveness to changes in customer needs.

The disadvantage of a business being market orientated is that regular changes in the appearance or function of a product (to meet changing tastes) may leave customers confused about what the brand really stands for.

Primary market research

Primary and secondary market research are the two ways in which a business can undertake market research. These are essential for any business aiming to be market orientated. They allow the business to gather data on customer desires in relation to a product or service and can help in forecasting potential customer demand.

Primary market research is data gathered first-hand, such as customer interviews, probably using specifically designed questionnaires and carried out for a specific business.

Primary market research can be undertaken in many different ways:

- **Observation** is where the business watches customers to see how they behave when purchasing (or choosing not to purchase) specific products or services. This method is time consuming and costly but can reveal customer views and feelings about a product that other methods cannot.
- **Online surveys** are an ICT method of asking customers questions about a product or service through the use of a range of websites, such as social media sites or a specific question and answer website. Online surveys are widely used by businesses as a way of capturing the views of existing and potential customers and have the added benefit of automatically feeding the results into a database that can collect all the answers. However, they have low response rates from potential customers, so can give a distorted picture of consumer opinion generally.
- **Face-to-face surveys** are personal interviews conducted face to face to obtain customer views on product or services. They are a costly but productive way to get detailed insights from an individual. This method is particularly useful for asking more emotional response-style questions about the product or service.
- **Focus groups** are groups of potential customers brought together to discuss their feelings about a product or market. Focus groups are a good way of getting detailed qualitative information about customer tastes and preferences, but again can be expensive compared with other types of methods, such as online surveys.

The advantages for a business of using primary market research are that it gathers up-to-date customer views about the product, and questions can be tailored to meet the individual needs of the business.

Primary market research Data gathered first-hand that are specifically designed and obtained for a specific business.

Exam tip

Accurate definitions are the key to a good mark when answering exam questions. If they are both precise and concise, it will save you time in the exam room.

The disadvantages of using primary market research are that it can be difficult to collect the data, it can take a long time to gather them, and it is expensive to carry out. Primary research may provide misleading results if the **sample size** is not large enough or is not chosen with care, or if the questions are worded so as to **bias** the answers in a particular direction.

Secondary market research

Secondary market research involves using data collected by someone else that have not been designed specifically for the business requiring the information.

Secondary market research can be obtained from a number of sources:

- Government statistics are available to all businesses and contain data such as **demographic trends**, for example the rate of rise in the number of under-fives expected over the next five years. These are free to obtain and usually free from bias. The disadvantages are that the data can be a year or two out of date and all businesses have access to the same information.
- Mintel and other commercial organisations publish market research reports on hundreds of customer products and services. The advantage of these reports is that they are specifically about a certain market, showing its current businesses and potential areas for new businesses to target their product or services at. The disadvantages are that the reports are available to any business, they are still not completely focused on specific questions to which the business might like to know the answers, and they are expensive to buy.
- The business's own data, such as sales figures and the number of customers visiting the business, can be used to help research what customers want from a product or service. The advantage of this research is that the business already has the data, so it is cheap and confidential. The disadvantage is that it may not answer the key questions a business has to ensure its products or services are successful.
- A competitor's data, for example publicly available sales and profit figures, can be used to help research how the competitor is performing in the market. The advantages of this research are that it is very cheap to obtain and shows rivals' performance in the market. The disadvantages are that every competitor can access it and the information available is very basic, so it is usually of little real value.

Advantages of a business using secondary market research are that it is time and cost effective because the data already exist and are either freely available or cheaper than if the same data were gathered by primary research methods.

Disadvantages of a business using secondary market research are that the business is not gathering its own information, first-hand, it is totally dependent on someone else's efforts, and the data may be inaccurate or biased, so using it to make business decisions is risky.

Exam tip

Data in the extract should be used to build your arguments about market trends, but remember to look at the bigger picture as well for high marks.

Sample size The amount of data collected by the business from customers or potential customers.

Bias Where the findings do not give a true reflection of the views of the target audience on the product or service.

Demographic trends Statistics showing how things are changing within the population, such as age, marital status, place of birth and household income.

Knowledge check 4

Explain how Walkers Snack Foods, famous for its range of crisps, might use market research if it decided to launch its first chocolate bar.

Exam tip

A risk with market research is that consumers struggle to look into the future. More than 100 years ago Henry Ford said that if he had asked the public, they would have asked for a faster horse rather than a car.

Knowledge check 5

Explain why bias may be a problem in research for a new product launch.

Market segmentation

Market segmentation involves dividing a market into smaller sets of customers, or segments, who have similar needs and interests. For example, a bank might segment its potential customers into those aged 18–24 in order to look at the needs and wants of those customers in terms of bank accounts.

Advantages for a business using market segmentation are that it creates separate products for each segment, which means the business can focus on how best to meet those customers' needs, and it can increase sales by allowing the business to identify areas of growth for products and services. The main disadvantage with segmentation is that producing a number of products to suit different tastes is expensive – and can make it difficult for any of them to make a profit.

Market positioning

Market mapping

Market mapping means creating a diagram that identifies all the products in the market using two key features, for example price and quality – see Figure 1. The aim is to spot a need or want that is not currently covered by products in the market and which can be exploited by the business. This is often called a 'gap in the market'.

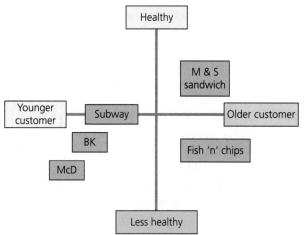

Figure 1 Example of a market map for fast food

Advantages for a business using market mapping are that it helps to spot gaps in the market that may lead to an exciting product innovation, and it allows the business to see what competitors are doing in the market in terms of products and services.

Disadvantages for a business using market mapping are that, even if a gap in the market is identified, it doesn't mean there will be any demand for a product created to fill this gap, and it is based on only two variables, so it can oversimplify the picture of the market, meaning business decisions are made on insufficient evidence.

Market segmentation Dividing a market into smaller sets of customers with similar needs and interests.

Market mapping The process of creating a diagram that identifies all the products in the market using two key features.

Knowledge check 6

What is the difference between market mapping and market segmentation?

Exam tip

Be careful not to confuse market mapping with market segmentation when completing an 'explain how' question.

Competitive advantage

Competitive advantage is a sustainable way to keep ahead of your competitors in the long term. This might be because your production efficiencies make you the lowest-cost supplier, e.g. Primark, or because customers believe your brand is differentiated clearly from others, e.g. BMW. The safer of these two positions is probably to be highly differentiated – after all, Coca-Cola has outsold Pepsi for the past 125 years.

Product differentiation

Product differentiation is actual or perceived features of a product or service that the business uses to convince customers to buy its product instead of those of competitors in the market.

Businesses use a variety of methods to differentiate their product or service, such as special product features, packaging and branding.

Advantages include focusing on telling customers what is different and better about the product, meaning customers are likely to buy it instead of others in the market. This can **add value** to the product, with customers then being willing to pay a higher price.

The only potential disadvantage of product differentiation is that the attempt to be different might add more to design and production costs than customers are willing to pay. At present this is true of hydrogen cell-powered cars (the Toyota Mirai is the same size as a Prius, but is priced almost three times higher at £60,000!).

> **Exam tip**
>
> Use concepts such as competitive advantage to help evaluate a business's strengths within its market and remember not to define a differentiated product simply as one that is different, as this will gain no marks.

Competitive advantage A way to keep your competitors at arm's length over a sustained period.

Added value The difference or perceived customer difference between the selling price and the cost of bought-in goods and services. The more exciting and original the features, the higher the value may be to the customer.

Summary

After studying this topic, you should be able to:
- describe what niche, mass and dynamic markets are and state their advantages and disadvantages
- discuss the differences between a niche and a mass market
- explain the difference between risk and uncertainty and the effect competition has on price and demand
- describe product and market differentiation and their advantages and disadvantages
- describe primary and secondary market research, including the advantages and disadvantages of different methods
- describe market positioning and market segmentation, including their benefits and drawbacks
- describe what is meant by competitive advantage and the advantages and disadvantages of product differentiation

■ The market

Demand

Demand is the amount of a good or service which customers buy at a given price and within a given time period. Demand is normally illustrated by a demand curve diagram, which has two axes. The *x*-axis, the horizontal line along the bottom of the diagram, represents the quantity of the goods or services being sold. The *y*-axis, running vertically from bottom to top, represents the price at which the goods are sold. The line drawn is called the demand curve and each point on the demand curve represents the amount of goods or services a customer is willing to buy at that price.

Factors leading to a change in demand

The demand for a good or service will go up if the price is cut. The demand for a good or service will go down if the price increases. Price is the only factor that moves demand up and down the demand curve. All other factors that change demand move the curve left or right of its starting position in Figure 2. This means there will be a new demand curve.

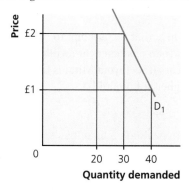

Figure 2 Demand curve

If the demand curve shifts to the left of its original position, it means demand for the product or service has decreased, as in Figure 3. The leftward shift means that at a price of £2, demand falls from 30 units to 20.

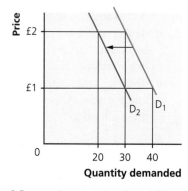

Figure 3 Demand curve showing shift to the left

If the demand curve shifts to the right of its original position, it means demand for the product or service has increased, as in Figure 4.

> **Exam tip**
>
> You need to be able to draw a demand curve diagram and to be able to explain what is happening to demand and why.

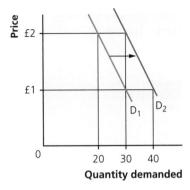

Figure 4 Demand curve showing shift to the right

The main factors that can lead to a change in demand are as follows:

■ Changes in the prices of **substitute goods**. If the price of one good increases, then demand for the substitute is likely to rise, meaning the demand curve will shift to the right for the substitute for the good – see Figure 5.

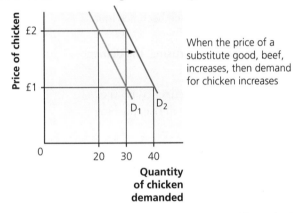

When the price of a substitute good, beef, increases, then demand for chicken increases

Substitutes Two goods that can be used for the same purpose, e.g. Cadbury's Dairy Milk and Galaxy chocolate.

Figure 5 Demand curve showing increase in demand for substitute good

■ Changes in the prices of **complementary goods**. If the demand for one good goes up, then demand for the complementary good will also rise, meaning the demand curve will shift to the right for both the good and the complementary good – see Figure 6.

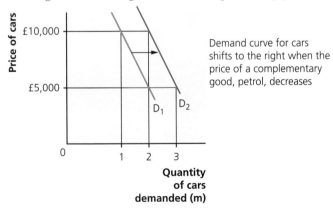

Demand curve for cars shifts to the right when the price of a complementary good, petrol, decreases

Complementary goods Goods that are used together, e.g. cars and petrol – if car prices fall, the demand for cars will rise, and so will the demand for petrol.

Figure 6 Demand curve showing increase in demand for complementary good

■ Changes in consumer incomes. If incomes increase, customers will buy more of the product or service, shifting the demand curve to the right – see Figure 7.

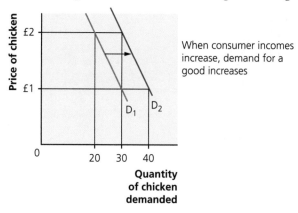

When consumer incomes increase, demand for a good increases

Figure 7 Demand curve showing increase in demand due to an increase in consumer incomes

■ Fashions, tastes and preferences. If a business's product or service becomes more fashionable, the demand curve will shift to the right.
■ Advertising and **branding**. If a business spends heavily on advertising, the demand curve should shift to the right, meaning more demand.

Demographics, such as population trends, can affect the demand curve. With the number of over-65s increasing, the demand for Stannah stairlifts will rise, pushing the demand curve to the right.

External shocks, such as a **recession** or sharp change in exchange rates, can also affect the demand curve. When the UK economy is in recession, the demand curve for most products shifts to the left as customers struggle with less disposable income – see Figure 8.

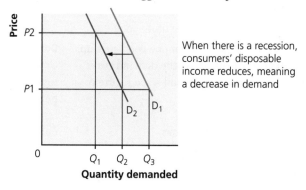

When there is a recession, consumers' disposable income reduces, meaning a decrease in demand

Figure 8 Demand curve showing a decrease in demand due to a recession

Another factor is seasonality, where some goods or services face a change in demand depending on the time of year they are sold. For example, the demand curve of ice cream will shift to the right with increased demand in the summer.

Branding The process involved in creating a unique name and image for a product in the customer's mind, mainly through advertising campaigns with a consistent theme.

Recession A period of temporary economic decline in a country, during which trade and industrial activity are reduced.

Exam tip

The demand for most products is affected by more than one factor. This can make it hard to judge which is the most important. Good exam answers are bold in selecting factors and backing them with supporting argument.

Supply

Supply is the amount of goods or services provided at a given price by all the companies within a market.

Supply is normally illustrated through the use of a supply curve diagram, as shown in Figure 9. The diagram has two axes. The *x*-axis represents the quantity of the goods or services being supplied. The *y*-axis represents the price at which the goods are supplied. Each point on the supply curve represents the amount of goods or services a business is willing to supply at that price.

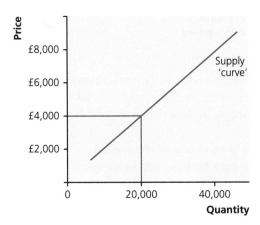

Figure 9 A supply curve

Factors leading to a change in supply

The supply curve slopes upwards because the higher the price, the more businesses will want to supply. A high selling price means high profits for the supplier, so companies may switch resources from other production to focus on the market with high prices/profits. The supply for a good or service will go down the lower the price, as businesses will be discouraged from creating more of their product if they may make less profit. Price is the only factor that moves supply up and down the supply curve.

All other factors that change supply shift the curve left or right of its starting position on the diagram. This means there will be a new supply curve. These factors include the following:

■ Changes in the **costs of production**, where the costs of making the product from raw materials go up or down. Where the costs of production increase, the supply curve will shift left and supply will reduce.
■ Introduction of new technology, which is likely to mean the business can create the product at a lower cost, encouraging greater supply. This means the supply curve will shift to the right and supply will increase – see Figure 10.

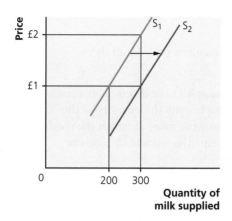

Figure 10 Supply curve shifting to the right due to introduction of new technology

- **Indirect taxes**, which are taxes on goods or services such as Value Added Tax on electricity or gas used by businesses in making or selling products or services. If indirect tax goes down, businesses will want to supply more of the product. This means the supply curve will shift to the right.
- **Government subsidies**, where the government gives money to a business to reduce its costs, normally of production. This means a business will supply more of the product, moving the supply curve to the right.
- **External shocks**, such as severe drought in farming areas. This will create shortages and therefore increase the cost to manufacturers of buying in raw materials. This means the supply curve will shift to the left – see Figure 11.

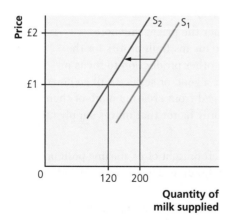

Figure 11 Supply curve shifting to the left due to an increase in raw material prices

Markets – how supply and demand affect each other

A diagram can be drawn that includes both supply and demand. The price at which the quantity demanded by customers is equal to the quantity supplied by businesses is called **equilibrium** – see Figure 12.

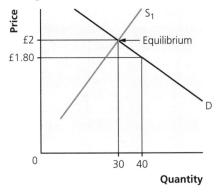

Figure 12 Equilibrium: where supply and demand meet

An example of a factor that affects supply and demand is an increase in demand caused by a rise in disposable income. The shift in the demand curve will be to the right as demand increases, raising the equilibrium price. As a result, the supply of the product will also increase as businesses want to produce more at the higher price. There is a movement up the supply curve creating a new equilibrium.

A change in supply can also affect supply and demand. For example, a reduction in the costs of production, such as lower wage costs for employees, would mean the business will produce more of the product, shifting the supply curve to the right. As the price of supply is now lower, there will be a greater demand for the product at the lower price.

There is a movement down the demand curve. This results in a new equilibrium, as shown in Figure 13.

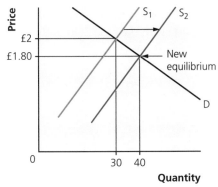

Figure 13 Where costs of production decrease, supply shifts right

Price elasticity of demand

Price elasticity of demand (PED) measures the responsiveness of demand to a change in price.

If a company's costs have risen, it naturally wants to push up its prices to compensate. But what would be the effect on customers? If prices were increased by 5%, would sales volumes fall by 1%, 5% or perhaps even 10%? Knowing the answer to this question is vital because it determines whether the 5% price rise boosts or actually diminishes the company's revenue. If a business is selling 1,000 units a week at £20 each and then decides to increase its price by £1 (5%), the possible effects would be as shown Table 1.

> **Price elasticity of demand** Percentage change in quantity demanded / percentage change in price.

Table 1 The effect on revenue of an increase in price

	Sales fall by 1%	Sales fall by 5%	Sales fall by 10%
New sales volume	990 units	950 units	900 units
New price	£21	£21	£21
New sales revenue	£20,790	£19,950	£18,900
Change in revenue (compared with £20,000)	+£790	−£50	−£1,100

So the effect on revenue of a 5% price rise depends on the price sensitivity of the product. If it is very price sensitive (sales fall by 10% when price rises by 5%), the price rise is self-defeating – it cuts revenue. In business, the term given for price sensitivity is price elasticity. If customers are making their purchasing decisions mainly on the basis of price, the price sensitivity/elasticity will be high. For a company, that's not good. If your products are highly price elastic, cost increases cannot easily be passed on to customers, so profits can easily be squeezed – and perhaps turn into losses.

It is important for a business to look at the amount of a good or service sold compared with the price it charges. To measure PED a formula is used:

$$PED = \frac{\text{percentage change in quantity demanded}}{\text{percentage change in price}}$$

For example, a business is looking at reducing its price to customers from £60 to £40. Sales are currently 15,000 but are predicted to reach 25,000 with the reduction in the price, as shown on the demand curve in Figure 14.

> **Exam tip**
>
> Remember to show your workings out and the formula in any 'calculate' question. Really importantly, do not forget the minus sign as doing so will lose you an easy mark.

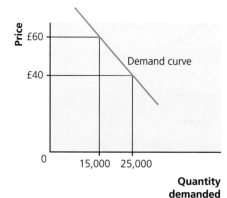

Figure 14 Price elasticity of demand calculation

Percentage change in demand = (25,000 − 15,000 = 10,000)/15,000 = 0.66×100 = 66%

Percentage change in price = (£40 − £60 = −£20)/£60 = −0.33×100 = −33%

Price elasticity of demand = 66%/−33% = −2

Conclusion: This means demand is very sensitive to the price of the product: demand is price elastic.

Interpretation of the values of price elasticity of demand

The values the calculation shows give a business an indication of how sensitive a product is to changes in price. The values are:

- If PED is between 0 and −1, this means price elasticity is low, probably because it is a well-differentiated, perhaps well-branded product. Demand is price inelastic.
- If PED = −1, this means the % change in demand is exactly the same as the % change in price. The percentage rise in price of the product would lead to exactly the same percentage fall in demand, leaving total revenue the same.
- If PED = −1 or more, this means demand is very sensitive to the price of the product: demand is price elastic. This must be an undifferentiated product, such as apples at a street market. If the price of the product went up 10%, demand might fall by 20%.

Exam tip

When reading the examiner's text, think about whether the featured product/ brand is price elastic or inelastic. Then use that insight to analyse how a business should set about pricing its product.

Factors influencing price elasticity of demand

There are various factors influencing price elasticity of demand:

- **The number of close substitutes.** The closer substitutes there are in the market, the more elastic is demand as customers find it easier to switch to another product.
- **The cost of switching between products.** If there are costs involved in switching to another product, then demand is more likely to be inelastic.
- **Whether the product is a luxury or essential to the customer.** Necessities tend to have an inelastic demand but luxury products tend to have a more elastic demand.
- **If the product is one that customers consume out of habit.** As customers become used to buying a product they become less sensitive to its price. This means the demand becomes more price inelastic and less sensitive to price increases.

Knowledge check 8

What is an advantage to a business such as Apple of a price inelastic good?

The significance of PED to a business

PED is important to a business as it helps it decide how consumers will react to a change in a product's price. If the product is sensitive to price, the business can decide to:

- cut costs instead of raising prices – this will mean more potential profit without disturbing demand
- cut the price to give a sharp boost to demand – this will increase revenue and may boost profit, especially if unit costs can be reduced by bulk buying

■ attempt to make the product more price inelastic – for example, use advertising and branding to make the product more desirable to the customer or add value to the product by adding new features to make it unique, i.e. give the product a competitive advantage. For example, smartphones have moved from being a luxury to being perceived as a necessity, with leading devices like the iPhone commanding very high prices while still attracting large demand (price inelastic).

Calculating total revenue and interpreting the relationship with demand

PED enables a business to calculate the revenue that can be earned at a particular price point for its product. **Total revenue** depends on the number of products sold and the price they are sold at for a specific period of time and can be worked out using the following calculation:

Total = Price × Quantity

By calculating total revenue for different price points the business can identify the point on the demand curve where revenue is maximised – see Table 2 and Figure 15. In order to ensure the most accurate predictions, the company could use market research to measure customers' views on price and likely demand.

Table 2 Total revenue = price × quantity demanded

Price (£)	Quantity demanded (Q)	Total revenue (P × Q)
10	6,000	60,000
20	5,000	100,000
30	4,000	120,000
40	3,000	120,000
50	2,000	100,000

In the above example the business would see that the best total revenue achieved is when the price is set between £30 and £40.

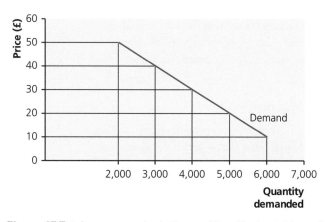

Figure 15 Total revenue calculation and its effect on demand

Exam tip

Beware of confusing price and income elasticity. And remember that there is no such thing as 'a product's elasticity'; an income elastic product can be price inelastic.

Total revenue The number of products sold times price in a given period of time.

Exam tip

Expect to be asked to do some basic maths as part of a question on calculating total revenue, and in particular know how to work out the percentage change in total revenue.

Income elasticity of demand

Income elasticity of demand (YED) measures the responsiveness of demand to a change in households' real income.

To measure YED, a formula is used:

$$\text{YED} = \frac{\text{percentage change in quantity demanded}}{\text{percentage change in income}}$$

Interpretation of the values of income elasticity of demand

Normal goods have a positive income elasticity of demand – see Figure 16. As a customer's income rises, more is demanded at each price. For example, if people are 3% better off, they tend to buy 3% more chocolate, giving chocolate an income elasticity of +1.

Let's consider a consumer who buys 20 music downloads per year on an income of £20,000. Following an increase in income to £40,000, the consumer buys 40 music downloads per year.

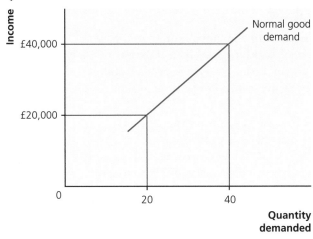

Figure 16 Income elasticity of demand calculation: normal goods

Income elasticity of demand = (change in quantity demanded/original quantity demanded) / (change in income/original income)

Percentage change in demand = (40 − 20 = 20)/20 = 1×100 = 100%

Percentage change in income = (£40,000 − £20,000 = £20,000)/£40,000 = 0.5×100 = 50%

Income elasticity of demand = 100%/50% = +2

Conclusion: The positive figure means that the good is a normal good. Because the answer is greater than 1, demand for the good, music downloads, responds more than proportionately to a change in income. This means the good is not a necessity such as food but is a relative luxury for the individual. This means demand is very sensitive to the price of the product – demand is elastic.

Exam tip

Income elasticity can be used to judge how severely a business would be affected by economic change – and is a fundamental part of any sales forecasting. Unfortunately, many students fail to see how valuable it is for answering questions.

Luxury goods and services have an income elasticity of demand of more than +1. This means that as people become better off, they buy lots more of these products, e.g. foreign holidays.

Inferior goods have a negative income elasticity of demand, meaning that demand falls as income rises. For example, a consumer buys 200 loaves of bread per year on an income of £40,000. Following an increase in income to £50,000, the consumer buys 180 loaves of bread per year.

Income elasticity of demand = (change in quantity demanded/original quantity demanded) / (change in income/original income)

Percentage change in demand = (180 − 200 = −20)/200 = −0.1×100 = −10%

Percentage change in income = (£50,000 − £40,000 = £10,000)/£40,000 = 0.25×100 = 25%

Income elasticity of demand = −10%/25% = −0.4

Conclusion: The negative figure means that the good is an inferior good. Because the answer is less than 1, demand for the good, loaves of bread, does not respond significantly to a change in income.

Factors influencing income elasticity of demand

The factors influencing income elasticity of demand are as follows:

- **The degree of attractiveness of the product to the consumer.** If an iPhone 7 is an absolute must, people will be determined to get it even if their incomes are being squeezed. So even though, objectively, an iPhone is a luxury, people's desires and brand loyalty may make it more of a necessity (with a low, positive income elasticity).
- **How large a proportion of household income is spent on the item.** For most people a new car is a major purchase that takes a big chunk out of the household budget. By contrast, spending on TV streaming services is a small proportion. So spending on TV streaming services is likely to be affected little by economic ups and downs. It will have a positive income elasticity, but at a low level (under +1). By contrast, a new car will be a luxury good, with a figure above +1.

The significance of income elasticity of demand (YED) to a business

YED is important as it helps managers decide how sensitive their product is in terms of demand when income changes. They can use that information to forecast sales. If, in 2017, the Chinese economy grows by 7%, sales of the Land Rover Evoque may grow by 28% because the Evoque has an income elasticity estimated at +4.

If a company's main product is a highly income-elastic luxury brand, the business can decide to:

- focus new product development on a value-for-money brand that will appeal to people feeling under financial pressure – then if sales of the luxury brand flag in a recession, there will still be strong sales from the 'inferior', value-for-money version
- keep focused purely on the luxury sector but be more cautious on the financial side, e.g. keeping an extra-strong cash flow position to cope with downturns in sales

Knowledge check 9

Give an example of a normal good.

Exam tip

Don't wait to be asked about a topic such as income elasticity. If you can use it to construct an argument that's relevant to the question, fire away.

Summary

After studying this topic, you should be able to:
- describe and interpret demand and supply and the factors that influence changes in demand and supply in relation to a business or market
- explain, calculate and interpret price elasticity of demand in a business context
- explain, calculate and interpret income elasticity of demand in a business context
- explain, calculate and interpret total revenue and its relationship with demand

■ Marketing mix and strategy

The **marketing mix** is the way the business controls four elements, called the 4 Ps, to ensure the product is suitable to potential customers: product, price, place and promotion. The secret to a successful marketing mix is to ensure that it is well integrated across the four elements and that the whole mix creates the right image to match the marketing opportunity that has been identified.

Product service/design

The design mix

The design mix consists of the function, aesthetics (looks) and costs of creating and manufacturing the product.

Good product design adds value and adds to brand image and loyalty. The three parts work together to create the product for the market as follows:
- **Function** is how effectively the product works: does a smartphone have great sound, a brilliant camera and long battery life? Is it reliable?
- **Aesthetics** are how the product appeals to the subjective views of customers in terms of how it looks, feels or smells. This can differentiate the product from others in the same market, creating more customer demand. Well made though the iPhone is, most people would say that its aesthetics mark it out as special.
- **Costs of creating the product** mean the costs involved in its manufacture and production. The product must be designed so that it can be produced cheaply enough to make a profit from sales to customers. Adding value in the production process helps to make sure the design of the product is more likely to be profitable.

> **Design mix** The combination of the three factors needed to create an effective design: function, aesthetics and costs.

Changes in the design mix

In order to ensure the product achieves the maximum profits for the business, the design mix needs to be changed to reflect the following:
- **Social trends** are the cultural values and practices of customers – they can be short or long term.
- **Concern over resource depletion** involves the recognition that certain raw materials being used in the design mix may be becoming rarer, so the product will need to be redesigned to do without such materials.

> **Exam tip**
>
> You should be able to identify and evaluate which aspect of the design mix is relevant to a question. However, remember that there are always downsides to design, such as extra costs, so look at the bigger picture.

- **Designing for waste management** means the design mix must be constantly focused on reducing the raw materials, energy or human resources used in production. Any waste material needs to be disposed of cheaply, so as technology develops, new methods of waste management will need to be incorporated into the production process. The aim is to keep production costs as low as possible to ensure the highest possible profit.
- **Re-use and recycling** of raw materials used to create the product can be emphasised to customers to add value to the product and differentiate it from competitors.
- **Ethical sourcing** means reducing the environmental impact of the creation of the product.

Branding and promotion

Types of promotion

Promotion is the way a business makes its products known to its current and potential customers. It is one of the 4 Ps that form the marketing mix.

Promotion means communicating to customers about the product and persuading them to purchase it. The combination of methods used to promote the product is called the **promotional mix**.

Which promotional methods are used depends on factors such as how long the product has been on sale, what the product is, competition in the market and the target market.

The main types of promotion are:
- **advertising**, through media such as television, newspapers and social media
- viral marketing, to advertise products to a large audience – consider the John Lewis department store YouTube video that had 1.25m hits for 'Monty the penguin'
- emotional marketing, to show how a product can enhance self-esteem and/or happiness – for example, Nike often uses sporting adverts to show the prowess of famous sports people, which plays to our emotions as we all aspire to be fit and healthy
- **public relations (PR) and sponsorship**, as a means of creating and maintaining a positive image of the business and/or product. One method used to do this is sponsorship, paying a celebrity or sports team to advertise products – for example, Liverpool football club is sponsored by Subway, the sandwich chain.

Types of branding

Branding is the process involved in creating a unique name and image for a product in the customer's mind, mainly through advertising campaigns with a consistent theme. Branding is part of promotion.

The main types of branding are:
- **product**, where the item has a unique logo or packaging which customers are familiar with, such as the Adidas logo
- **personal**, where the product is associated with celebrities or sports personalities, who endow the product with the positive values they display in their public image

Viral marketing The method of creating advertising that is memorable and attention-grabbing for use in social media campaigns.

Emotional marketing Any advertising that aims to appeal directly to customers' needs and aspirations.

- **corporate**, where the business advertises a broad range of positive images about itself in the hope that the products will have the same virtues – for example, Apple's corporate brand attempts to instil innovation and creativity across all its products

All these types of branding aim to differentiate the product from others in the market.

Ways to build a brand

The main ways to build a brand are through the different methods of promotion mentioned earlier in the guide. These methods create a unique selling point (USP), which is something about the product that makes it different from other products in the market.

To enhance the brand and ensure it is constantly relevant to customers, the business must ensure that promotion reflects current social trends and the way the product meets customer expectations.

Social media can be used to try to build a connection between the business and the consumer. The milkshake business Shakeaway, for example, pays a lot of attention to its Facebook page and blogs, encouraging customers to suggest new flavours and taking care to answer points and queries. The hope is to get customers to feel part of something instead of being outsiders. Every company craves a fraction of the connection between a football club and its fans – Shakeaway wants customers who 'love' its milkshakes just as Foxes fans love Leicester City.

The benefits of strong branding

The benefits of a strong brand are:

- added value, which means enhancing the gap between the production cost and the selling price. Customers can perceive the product as better than rivals due to the brand image, thus enhancing brand loyalty. Companies often respond to their customers' loyalty by putting up the price!
- being able to charge premium prices – thanks to a stronger brand image, customers are willing to pay a higher price for the product because of its perceived enhanced quality
- reduced elasticity of demand – the strength of the brand may make customers less sensitive to price increases.

Pricing strategies

Types of pricing strategy

Price is part of a business's marketing mix and one of the 4 Ps. Price is the amount the business charges the customer for the product or service. The business can work out the price for which it will sell its product to a customer by looking at various factors. These include the costs of producing the product, its brand image, the target market and the target customers. This will help the business form a pricing strategy.

Unique selling point An attribute that makes a product stand out from other products in the market.

Exam tip

The specification talks of 'the benefits of strong branding', but benefits to whom? Yes, to the brand owner, but what about the consumer (paying high prices)? And what of a new, small company, trying to break into a market dominated by a strong brand? In this connection, the word 'benefit' needs careful evaluation.

Knowledge check 12

How does Nike's sponsorship of sports personalities such as the footballer Cristiano Ronaldo allow the company to add value to its range of sportswear?

There are various types of strategy.

Cost-plus pricing is where the business adds together the costs of the raw materials, labour and overheads for a product. This gives the cost per unit, also known as unit cost. The business then adds a mark-up percentage (to create a profit margin) in order to arrive at the price of the product. Cost-plus pricing is easy to calculate and a price increase can be justified when costs increase. However, it ignores price elasticity of demand and how sensitive the product is to rises in price; implicitly it is a product-rather than market-orientated method of pricing.

Price skimming means the business sets a high price before competitors come into the market or when the new product is believed to be superior to others on the market. Apple is known to use this method. Price skimming allows for greater profit from customers prepared to pay the premium price for the new product, often called 'early adopters'. However, sometimes the strategy breaks down as other competitors enter the market.

Penetration pricing involves the business setting a relatively low initial price to attract new customers. This is to encourage customers to switch to the new product to achieve a high market share. However, profit levels are likely to be low and starting at a low price may make it difficult for the product to establish a quality reputation.

Predatory pricing is where prices are deliberately set very low by a dominant business in the market in order to drive competitors out of the market or out of business. It is illegal under competition law, but it is very hard to prove that low prices are intended to damage others. Consumers love a price war, so it is difficult for competition authorities to step in and stop one.

Competitive pricing means the business must accept the going market price as determined by the forces of demand and supply and other similar products in the market. Such a business is known as a 'price taker' as it has to charge what others in the market do for their products. It implies that the business has a weak brand and its products lack differentiation.

Psychological pricing means the price is set to make the customer believe the product is cheaper than it really is. Pricing in this way is intended to attract customers who are looking for 'value'. Instead of charging £10.25, a business may charge £9.99, to avoid going through the £10 psychological price barrier. It may seem trivial but it can be important. No one wants to pay £1 for a chocolate bar, so 99p becomes the psychological price ceiling.

Factors that determine the most appropriate pricing strategy

The factors that help a business decide the most appropriate pricing strategy include:

- USP – a product with a unique selling point is differentiated from the rest of the market and has a clear competitive advantage
- price elasticity of demand
- level of competition – if there are many similar products then a business will need to use competitive pricing

Knowledge check 13

Why might Huawei, a new competitor to Apple, have to charge less for its smartphone than Apple?

Exam tip

Examiners love terminology. If you can distinguish clearly between the different pricing methods, you will be able to write far stronger arguments.

- strength of brand – if the business has a well-established and positive image, its products are likely to command a premium price, a higher price than competitors, for example Rolex watches
- the stage in the product life cycle – if the product is relatively new and innovative, price skimming may be adopted to gain maximum profit; later on, the business may need to switch to a competitive pricing approach
- costs and the need to make a profit – if the key to a business's survival is to ensure it makes a profit from each sale of the product, it may need to use cost-plus pricing
- online sales – customers can easily check the prices of a product sold at a variety of online and physical stores, which means that a business may have an online price that is based on competitors' pricing

Price comparison sites appear to give pricing transparency and therefore show who is offering the cheapest product. This should encourage a business to adopt competitive pricing. Unfortunately, many price comparison sites are merely sales outlets, pushing the products of those businesses that have paid for a listing.

Distribution

Distribution channels

Distribution channels are ways to get finished products to customers. The main methods of distributing the product to the customer are:

- **producer** to **wholesaler** to **retailer** to customer – where the wholesaler buys products in bulk from many producers of goods, storing and breaking them up into small batches for sale to retailers
- producer to retailer to customer – the producer sells the goods directly to the retailer, missing out the wholesaler. The retailer avoids the wholesaler's mark-up, but has to buy in huge bulk – perhaps a whole container-load. This is fine for Sainsbury's or B&Q, but not an option for a corner shop.
- producer to consumer – the producer of the product sells directly to the customer, missing out both the wholesaler and the retailer. This allows the producer to retain all the profits from the sale of its products. The customer is likely to be able to buy the product at a lower price than with other methods of distribution. This has always been important in some areas of retailing but today is transformed by the potential of e-commerce, that is selling online.

The key to a product's success and the business producing the most possible profit is choosing the best distribution channel. This process should take into account:

- customer choice or convenience – businesses may wish to choose a number of distribution methods to maximise the number of customers they sell to, for example physical retail outlets and online selling of the same product
- the image a business wishes to create – for a new organic yoghurt, distribution through independent grocers and posh sandwich shops will be better for the long-term image than rushing to get stocked by Tesco
- social trends where customers' buying habits change, such as the move away from physical grocery shopping to online shopping with delivery to the customer's door

Knowledge check 14

What type of brand can adopt a premium price?
....

Producer A business that makes, grows or supplies goods or commodities for sale.

Wholesaler A business that acts as a link between the producer and retailer; it buys in bulk and sells to resellers rather than to customers.

Retailer A business that sells goods or services directly to the customer.

- online distribution where the move from e-commerce to m-commerce (mobile commerce using smartphones) is accelerating a process that is starting to threaten the once comfortable existence of high street shops
- changing product to a service where the business technology means that customers no longer wish to purchase a physical item such as a CD but take delivery of their music through a download digital service such as Spotify or iTunes. Businesses need to adapt to this type of dynamic market to keep a competitive advantage.

Exam tip

Place (distribution) has sometimes been called the 'silent P' because students so underestimate its importance within the mix. Try to link distribution to other elements of the marketing mix in your answer.

Marketing strategy

The product life cycle

The product life cycle describes the stages a product goes through from conception until it is finally removed from the market – see Figure 17. Not all products reach this final stage – some continue to grow while others rise and fall.

The main stages of the product life cycle are:
- **introduction** – researching, developing and then launching the product
- **growth** – when sales are increasing at their fastest rate
- **maturity** – when sales are near their highest level but the rate of growth is slowing down
- **decline** – the final stage of the cycle, when sales begin to fall

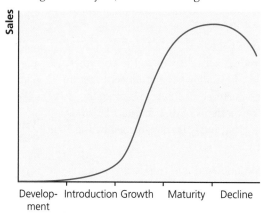

Figure 17 The product life cycle

The business can determine a product's point in the product life cycle by looking at the sales of the product compared with previous sales. As products cost a lot of money to design and manufacture there are a number of ways a business can attempt to keep sales as high as possible, known as **extension strategies**. Common extension strategies include:
- reformulating the product to position it more clearly towards a slightly different market, e.g. the Mini car, which used to appeal only to younger

Exam tip

The product life cycle is such an obvious model that few students take it seriously. In fact, it is a great basis for impressive analysis, with the potential for a debate about different pricing methods at different stages in the life cycle.

Exam tip

Students sometimes give examples of extension strategies that are really short-term tactics, such as a price promotion. To be a strategy it has to focus on the medium-long term, i.e. years, not weeks or months.

drivers but is now posher and more comfortable and therefore has broader market appeal

- changing the promotional focus, such as when the advertising for Johnson's Baby Powder switched from babies to mums ('If it's kind to babies' bottoms it'll be kind to your skin too') – this gave the brand an extension strategy with higher sales than the original marketing plan had envisaged

The Boston Matrix

A **product portfolio** is the term given to the full range of products and brands produced by a business.

A product portfolio can be analysed using the **Boston Matrix** in order for a business to decide on its spending priorities regarding product development and promotion.

The Boston Matrix places products into one of four different areas, based on:

- low or high market share
- whether the product is in a sector with high or low market growth

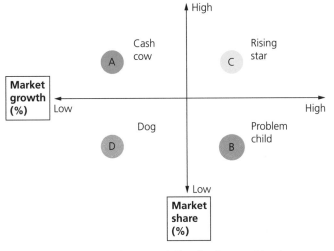

Figure 18 Product portfolio: the Boston Matrix

The four categories of the Boston Matrix, shown in Figure 18, are as follows:

- **Rising stars** have a strong share of a high-growth market. This makes them hugely valuable. They are likely to be profitable today and potentially even more so in the future. Companies are keen to invest in rising stars to maximise their huge potential.
- **Cash cows** are low-growth products with a high market share. These are mature, successful products with little need for investment.
- A **'problem child'** is a product with a low market share operating in a high-growth market. It might be a recently launched brand. It may have potential with the right investment behind it.
- **Dogs** are products that have a low market share in low-growth markets. Dogs may generate enough cash to be worth keeping going, but they are rarely worth investing in.

Knowledge check 15

The Apple iPhone 5s adopted which type of strategy related to the product life cycle?

Boston Matrix Analyses a company's product portfolio in relation to the rate of market growth and the level of market share.

Exam tip

Like all models, the Boston Matrix simplifies a complex world. Cadbury could treat its Dairy Milk brand as a cash cow, but experience teaches it that the brand still benefits from investment rather than simply being 'milked'.

The Boston Matrix is used to decide how to allocate marketing resources. Instead of spending equally on all products, a business might 'milk' its cows to provide the cash to support the rising stars and problem children.

Marketing strategies for different types of market

Businesses may try to market their products in different ways depending on the market they are in.

Niche marketing aims to market a product to a small group of the larger market. Using a niche marketing strategy makes a product easily differentiated from other products in the market, so in the short term it can avoid competition. However, as the market is comparatively small there is little room for competition, so any other business entering the market may reduce profits.

Mass marketing aims to market the product to a large part of the market. This means the product may not be differentiated as significantly as a niche market product in terms of features. Products are available to a wide target audience, so this spreads the risk to the business. However, there will be a greater number of competitors offering products that are very similar, so the risk is that the business may be forced to compete more on price, thus reducing profits.

Business-to-business (B2B) marketing is where a business is selling to another business rather than an ordinary householder, for example JCB selling a digger to a construction company. In B2B marketing, branding tends to be relatively unimportant – business buyers want high-quality products at good prices. So pricing and other strategies have to be tailored to the business buyer's needs.

Business-to-consumer (B2C) marketing is selling the product to the general public. The marketing emphasis is on branding and image – though of course customers want well-designed, well-made products. The buying process is focused on emotional issues and is very short. For example, an item of clothing is well understood by the customer and may be bought due to its brand, such as Chanel, and the aspirational image such products have for customers.

> **Exam tip**
> Really take notice if an exam paper features a B2B business, then tailor your answer to that specific issue.

Developing customer loyalty

The ultimate achievement in business is to change customer behaviour to make customers truly loyal to your brand. It is Apple's achievement in the smartphone market and Nike's achievement in sportswear. It makes customers less price sensitive and the product more price inelastic. This can be done through a number of marketing methods:

- The product needs to be designed to make a statement, i.e. not just featuring a Nike 'Swoosh' but also having its own style.

- Branding will help customers associate with the product and emphasise aspirational aspects of the product where appropriate.
- Customer service needs to be of high priority to the business in terms of both selling the product and dealing with customers after the sale.
- The product needs to be distributed to meet customers' needs.
- Companies that struggle to achieve real customer loyalty fall back on 'loyalty' cards to try to achieve repeat purchase. In effect, this means paying customers to be 'loyal' – a poor substitute for the real thing.

Summary

After studying this topic, you should be able to:
- describe the marketing mix, price, promotion, product and place/distribution
- discuss the advantages and disadvantages related to the marketing mix in the context of a business or market
- describe the product life cycle and the Boston Matrix, including their benefits and drawbacks to a business
- describe different marketing strategies for different markets
- describe how a business can develop customer loyalty

■ Managing people

Approaches to staffing

Staff are a key resource for any business as they provide a lot of the physical and creative work that both makes the product and sells it to the target customer.

Staff as an asset, staff as a cost

There are two ways a business views staff:
- as an asset, where the business treats the workers as a resource that needs to be developed and invested in, in order for them to provide the biggest return to the business
- as a cost, where the business views staff like any other expense that is incurred in creating the product or service

Businesses can view staff as both a cost and an asset in order to maximise the efficient and effective use of human resources within the business.

Flexible workforce

A business can reduce staffing costs by creating more flexible working.

Multi-skilling is the process of training employees so that they are able to undertake several different jobs within the business. Multi-skilling employees means they are able to take on many roles and thus can cover for staff absences or can cover rises and falls in demand from customers. However, staff might be more productive staying in one, specialist role – so multi-skilling may harm efficiency.

Multi-skilling Training employees to do several different jobs/skills within the business.

Part-time staff work shorter hours than full-time staff. Hours can be tailored to suit times of higher demand from customers, such as when high street shops are busier at the weekend. However, it may be that 24 part-time staff are less efficient than 12 full-timers, as the part-timers may be less well trained.

Temporary staff are employed by the business for a specific period of time only, either to cover periods of higher demand or to cover staff who are not able to work for a short period of time. The business is able to keep the costs low in only paying for the period of time that the member of staff is needed. However, it will take time for the new member of staff to become productive as they will need to be trained.

Flexible hours are where staff vary the hours they work to meet both the needs of the business and to some extent their own needs. The business can match staff working hours to periods of demand from customers. This is the staffing basis of companies such as the taxi firm Uber.

Zero-hours contracts are where the business does not guarantee any work to the employee until they can see that the demand is there to need them. The business can match demand from customers with the employees to meet that demand very precisely, reducing costs. However, employees become demotivated as they may feel undervalued, particularly if they do not get regular hours.

Homeworking involves the employee carrying out all or part of their job at home without the need to attend the business's premises. The business can reduce the cost of providing space for employees to work. However, staff may be less productive as the business is not able to supervise the work directly.

Outsourcing is where the business finds another business to supply components or services that employees may have undertaken in the past. Outsourcing allows the business to concentrate on fewer tasks and become more productive. However, the business does not have direct control of outsourced employees, so quality may suffer. The experience of outsourcing from the public to the private sector is very unsatisfactory, with many examples of a greater focus on profit than on providing a proper service. For example, the 2012 Olympic security was outsourced to a private company, which failed to deliver the service required in the contract and overcharged the government for the service it did provide.

The differences between dismissal and redundancy

Dismissal occurs when an employer makes someone leave their job due to dissatisfaction with their performance, such as when the employer has decided the employee's performance is inadequate or that they have broken a clause within their employment contract. Dismissal is likely to affect just one employee whereas redundancy may affect many employees.

Redundancy is where employees have to leave because their job function is no longer needed by the business. The business is required to pay compensation for the loss of the employee's job, whereas dismissal has no such requirement. Redundancy is likely to be due to changes in technology or working practices, or because the business is closing down; with dismissal the business will still be operating as normal.

Exam tip

Try to see the approaches to staffing in a question as an argument between cost savings for the business in the short term and the effect of motivation of staff in the longer term. Relate these two issues to the stimulus material to impress the examiner.

Knowledge check 16

Why might a discount supermarket such as Aldi decide to multi-skill its workforce?

Employer–employee relationships

Businesses have two main approaches to managing their relationships with employees, known as **bargaining**.

The **individual approach** is where a business and an employee negotiate an individual's terms and conditions of employment. This can include such issues as pay, holidays, bonuses, any introduction of new working practices and other changes in the workplace.

The individual approach can reduce conflicts between the two parties as they discuss the issues directly and understand each other's position on the employment contract. However, the business is often in a dominant position to dictate the terms of the negotiations, so the employee may not get the contract they want.

Collective bargaining is where a business negotiates with representatives of employees, such as trade unions, regarding the terms and conditions of employment. The negotiations will be about exactly the same issues as those in the individual approach but for many more employees.

Collective bargaining allows the business to potentially save time and money by negotiating with a small number of representatives rather than with all employees. Employees have more bargaining power as a large group than as an individual. However, the process is slower and more expensive as there are more terms and conditions for the wide range of employees represented.

Recruitment, selection and training

Recruitment and selection process

Recruitment and selection is the process of finding and hiring the best-qualified candidate for a job opening, in a timely and cost-effective manner. Recruitment takes place through a selection process, which is the series of steps taken to shortlist then choose the right employee for the job that is vacant within the business.

Recruitment and selection is important to a business to ensure it has the right employees with the correct skills, character and attitudes to ensure the products and services are created and/or sold to gain the highest profit. The process can consist of analysing what skills are needed for the job (job analysis), then issuing a job description with these skills and a profile of the type of person needed (person specification). The job is normally advertised and candidates are interviewed and selected based on who most closely meets the description and specification.

The longer and more detailed the process, the costlier to the business, but the more likely it is to get the best employee for the job.

Internal and external recruitment

The business can choose two ways to recruit new employees.

Internal recruitment is where the business looks to fill the job vacancy from within its existing workforce. This is likely to represent a promotion for an employee, giving them more authority and better pay. This is cheaper and quicker than external recruitment – for example, there is no need to advertise in the media and employees are likely to see this as career progression and become more motivated to work harder.

> **Knowledge check 17**
>
> Name one difference between redundancy and dismissal.

> **Exam tip**
>
> A question on redundancy will normally need a discussion about employees as a cost.

> **Exam tip**
>
> When considering recruitment, a powerful line of thought is to compare a focus on skills and experience with a focus on character and attitudes. Pret a Manger hires positive-thinking, ambitious people – not necessarily those with experience.

However, too much focus on internal recruitment might preclude new, fresh thinking from being brought into the business. There is a balance to be struck. It is not feasible that all recruitment could be done internally, nor would it be desirable. Even FC Barcelona buys players from other clubs.

External recruitment is when the business looks to fill the vacancy with an applicant from outside the business. New employees are more likely to bring new ideas to the business, but in the short term it will take time to get outsiders to really understand the workings and culture of the organisation. It also takes longer to complete the process than with internal recruitment and will be costlier, as the vacancy will be advertised in the media, for example.

Training of employees

Training is the process whereby an individual acquires new skills and knowledge or improves on those they already have. Training of a new employee will often start with induction training, which introduces the individual to the business. Job-specific training will then be used to improve an individual's abilities to contribute more to their employer.

On-the-job training is where employees are trained while carrying out an activity, often at their place of work. This is cost effective for the business as the employee is learning while working. However, it is reliant on the time another employee has available to conduct the training, so the training might not be thorough. Furthermore, the new employee is trained only to the same standard as the person they are learning from, so potentially they could pick up bad habits as well as good ones.

Off-the-job training involves employees being trained away from the job at a different location, for example a Tesco store manager attending a computer course at Microsoft's offices. This type of training offers a wider range of skills or qualifications than that based just on the business's field of expertise and is likely to be of a high quality as it is delivered by experts in the relevant field. However, the travel and course costs of sending the employee to another place are an extra business expense.

> **Exam tip**
>
> A good method of evaluating on- and off-the-job training is to look at how both types might interfere with a business's day-to-day operations. Taking an employee off a production line to train them could have a massive impact on the whole factory.

Organisational design

Structure

A business needs to ensure it is organised so that it can efficiently meet the needs and wants of customers who purchase its product or service.

The **hierarchy** of a business is the order or levels of management in it, from its lowest to highest rank. The business hierarchy will show the **chain of command**, which is the line of authority from the top down to the bottom of the organisation.

Span of control is the number of employees working directly under a manager. The span of control can be described as either wide or narrow. A wide span of control (see Figure 19) means that employees will have greater decision-making powers in the business and this may improve their levels of job satisfaction. However, the fact that each manager is responsible for many subordinates may add to the stress they feel at work.

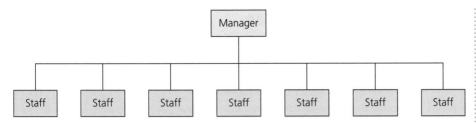

Figure 19 Wide span of control – one manager, many staff

Knowledge check 18

Why might a business such as McDonald's operate a narrow span of control in its restaurants?

A narrow span of control means that employees will have fewer decision-making powers as there will be more managers supervising a smaller number of employees – see Figure 20. Employees are closely supervised, resulting in better control of their activities, both individually and when working as a larger group. The closer supervision should help in minimising mistakes – essential in some businesses such as the manufacture of aircraft engines. However, it can lead to employees who are less motivated and less willing to think creatively about their job. Many people dislike the feeling of being over-supervised.

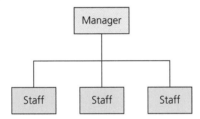

Figure 20 Narrow span of control – one manager, few staff

Centralised and decentralised organisational structures

Centralisation of an organisation means that decision making is kept at the centre, not passed down to individual outlets/stores or individuals. Junior staff cannot complete tasks until managers give authority for them to do so.

Senior managers have more control over the business and can make standardised decisions that must be applied everywhere. This helps cost efficiency when the business benefits from the bulk purchase of raw materials. However, there is too little flexibility to allow adjustments to variations in local tastes, and ambitious, creative junior staff will look for a job elsewhere.

Decentralisation means a business places the authority to make decisions with operating units such as stores or factories. Local managers are given plenty of scope to make decisions that may be quite bold and unexpected. (Chicken McNuggets came from a franchisee's idea, which was then adopted worldwide.) However, the local decision maker is looking at only a small part of the business and the business is less likely to benefit from cost savings of buying raw materials in bulk.

Exam tip

When evaluating centralisation or decentralisation, remember to relate this to motivational and leadership theories.

Exam tip

It can be useful to analyse the different types of organisational structure through Herzberg's two-factor theory (see pp. 38–9): motivation through job enlargement evaluated against job security.

Tall, flat and matrix organisational structures

A **tall** organisational structure has many levels of hierarchy and the span of control is narrow. Communication through the business takes a long time. As there are many management layers, promotion prospects come along every few years, potentially keeping staff hungry. However, communication takes a long time, so the business is less responsive to changes needed to remain competitive. Employees can become demotivated as the many layers of management make decision making slow and cautious.

A **flat** organisational structure has few levels of hierarchy and a wide span of control. Vertical communication takes less time and is therefore more effective and more motivating. As communication takes a short amount of time, the business is more responsive to changes needed to remain competitive. Employees can feel motivated as they are given more authority, called **delegation**, to make decisions, so productivity may increase.

Figure 21 shows the tall vs. the flat organisational structure.

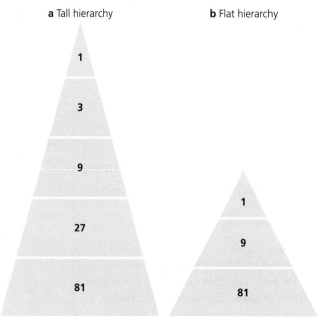

a Tall hierarchy **b** Flat hierarchy

Figure 21 Organisational structures with the number of people at each level of the hierarchy

A matrix organisational structure involves individuals working across teams and projects as well as within their own department. For example, an employee from the Finance and Human Resources department will work with designers and production staff on a new product for a customer. Table 3 gives an example of this kind of working.

A **matrix** structure can help to break down department barriers, improving communication across the entire organisation and encouraging employees to share ideas, which can make the business more efficient. However, members of project teams may find they have divided loyalties as they report to two managers, and it takes time for team members to get used to working in this kind of structure, meaning productivity can suffer.

Table 3 Matrix organisational structure

	Marketing	Operations	Finance	Human resources
	Marketing manager	Operations manager	Finance manager	Human resources manager
Project A (Team leader)	Marketing Team (A)	Operations Team (A)	Finance Team (A)	Human resources Team (A)
Project B (Team leader)	Marketing Team (B)	Operations Team (B)	Finance Team (B)	Human resources Team (B)
Project C (Team leader)	Marketing Team (C)	Operations Team (C)	Finance Team (C)	Human resources Team (C)
Project D (Team leader)	Marketing Team (D)	Operations Team (D)	Finance Team (D)	Human resources Team (D)

Exam tip
Look at the exam stimulus material to spot which structure seems to be operated by the business and whether this is the most appropriate. Examiners credit students who can suggest a better approach for a business in the stimulus material.

Motivation in theory and practice

It is important for a business to motivate employees as this can lead to higher productivity, more creativity and ultimately greater profits. Employees who are not motivated risk having a negative effect on the business, such as being absent more often from work, working below their maximum and providing customers with second-class service.

Motivational theories

There are four theories on motivation to consider.

Taylor's scientific management states that employees are mainly motivated by pay. Taylor also believed employees need close supervision and should do only small tasks they can repeat to become efficient at them. Taylor believed by paying workers a **piece rate**, this would motivate them to do as many pieces as possible.

Piece rate An amount paid for each task done.

Workers are encouraged to increase productivity, leading to more pay for themselves and higher output and lower costs for the business. However, Taylor treated employees like machines, leading to repetitive, boring jobs, potentially demotivated staff and high **labour turnover**.

Mayo came to believe that employees are motivated not just by money but also by social needs (something that Taylor ignored). This is called the **human relations theory** of motivation, which encourages managers to take a greater interest in workers as people.

Labour turnover The rate at which staff leave and have to be replaced.

By communicating with them, valuing their opinions and encouraging teamwork, there could be greater personal satisfaction, higher motivation and greater involvement in the business. This leads to greater productivity and working in teams encourages more creative problem solving to achieve the business's objectives. However, employees do not always have the same objectives as the business and communication between employees and managers is not always positive, for example when employees are made redundant. Therefore, motivation levels may not rise among all employees and productivity gains may be small.

Maslow's hierarchy of needs theory states that there are five levels of human needs which employees need to have fulfilled at work – see Figure 22. The needs are structured into a hierarchy and only once lower-level needs are fully met do higher needs start to matter.

Figure 22 Maslow's hierarchy of needs

Maslow's theory allows the business to create an environment for employees that satisfies many different needs, meaning a greater level of motivation for many staff, ultimately leading to higher productivity and increased profits. However, many critics suggest that esteem needs and self-actualisation can never be achieved in a job such as that of a street sweeper or toilet attendant.

Herzberg's two-factor theory of motivation says there are certain factors that a business could introduce that would directly motivate employees to work harder (motivators). Examples include responsibility, achievement and recognition for achievement. A separate set of factors (hygiene factors) is significant only when something is wrong. Professor Herzberg said pay was not a motivator, but if people feel underpaid, that gnaws away at them, causing job dissatisfaction and the likelihood of a dramatic response – perhaps pushing for strike action or being hostile in the workplace.

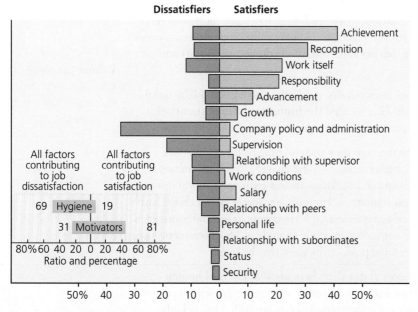

Figure 23 Comparison of Herzberg's satisfiers and dissatisfiers

Knowledge check 19

Name one benefit of Google using Maslow's theory of motivation for those employees designing new products.

Exam tip

Always start an exam answer on motivation with an academic definition, such as Professor Herzberg's. He defined motivation as 'doing something because you want to do it'.

Exam tip

Motivational theories can be used in many evaluative questions, particularly where there is a focus on reducing costs or improving quality. Remember, staff often provide the creative driving force behind a business, so costs and quality often suffer because the business forgets that motivating staff is key to achieving business objectives.

Looking at Figure 23 it can be seen that the dissatisfiers in Herzberg's theory demotivate employees, the biggest source of dissatisfaction being company policy and administration. The satisfiers give employees different levels of motivation, with achievement being the greatest. The key shows that hygiene factors contribute to dissatisfaction of up to 69% if absent from the workplace. Motivators can achieve greater satisfaction of up to 81% if employers enhance these factors in the workplace.

Herzberg's theory suggests businesses should focus on giving employees challenging, meaningful tasks leading to job satisfaction. This would encourage greater motivation and perhaps boost productivity. The theory warns against attempts to incentivise people to work hard just for the money. People's hygiene factors should be met, not manipulated.

Financial and non-financial ways to motivate employees

Financial incentives to improve employee performance include:

- piecework
- commission, where a payment is made as a percentage of the value of the good or service sold
- bonus, an extra payment made to recognise the contribution to a business
- profit share, where the more profit the business makes, the greater share of the profit the worker receives
- performance-related pay, a business's attempt to link pay to increased productivity by the employee

Taylor's theory of motivating employees is based on financial incentives, while Maslow's theory sees these as basic needs and Herzberg regards them as hygiene factors.

Non-financial techniques to improve employee performance include:

- delegation, where managers give responsibility for a task to an employee
- consultation, where employees will be asked for their views on business-related issues, though managers may not act on them
- empowerment, where official authority is given to employees to make decisions and control their own activities
- team working, where employees work in small groups with a common aim
- flexible working, which is a way of working that suits an employee's needs
- job enrichment, where employees are given greater responsibility and recognition by extending their role in the production process
- job rotation, where jobs or tasks are changed from time to time to reduce boredom and to provide greater labour flexibility
- job enlargement, where an employee will be given more work to do which is similar to their current role

Non-financial incentives can be linked to all of the theorists on motivation of employees except Taylor. For Maslow they tend to satisfy the higher-level needs and Herzberg suggested job enrichment as the key to human motivation.

Knowledge check 20

How could profit sharing be used at supermarket Morrisons to improve the overall profits of the business?

Knowledge check 21

How can job rotation on the BMW Mini production line help the business improve the quality of its products?

Leadership

The difference between management and leadership is that it is the manager's job to plan, organise and coordinate, while it is the leader's job to set clear goals, then help managers see how to achieve them.

Leadership styles

Leadership may inspire creativity and risk taking in a way management does not. Yet many successful leaders are never heard of, such as the boss of Costa Coffee (who took the business from 6 stores to 2,000). Quiet bosses are often the best.

There are various types of leadership style.

The **autocratic leader** makes all the decisions independently of employees. This may be a leader who shares Taylor's attitude to staff. Communication tends to be top down, with little delegation of tasks. Decision making is quickly put into practice throughout the business, with no consultation with employees. However, employees can feel undervalued as they have no say in how decisions are made, leading to demotivated staff and possible loss of productivity.

Under the **paternalistic leader**, more attention is given to the social needs and views of workers. The leader is interested in workers' wellbeing and acts as a father figure. They consult employees over issues and listen to their feedback or opinions, but any decisions are made by the leader. The style is closely linked with Mayo's and Maslow's views of motivation. Employees can feel more motivated as they believe their views are recognised and they understand why decisions are made, leading to improved productivity. However, there is little delegation and opportunities for employees to influence decisions may be quite limited.

The **democratic leader** encourages others to participate in decision making through consultation, often acting on the majority opinion on an issue. A democratic leader also favours delegation, i.e. passing decision-making authority down the hierarchy. This style is linked to Herzberg's theory on motivation. Employees will be more likely to be committed to decisions made within the business. However, consultation-based decisions tend to take a long time to make, meaning the business is not as responsive to changes in customer needs.

With the **laissez-faire leader**, indecision or absence at the top creates a decision-making vacuum which is filled by more junior staff. This sometimes happens in a school where the head is retiring in the coming summer and lets things start to slip. Fortunately, the vacuum allows employees to be at their most resourceful and creative – sometimes identifying new solutions to old problems. However, there may be little incentive for employees to work hard and lines of communication can be confused, leading to lower productivity and inconsistent delivery of the product to customers.

> **Knowledge check 22**
>
> Name a difference between autocratic and laissez-faire types of leadership.

> **Exam tip**
>
> Leadership often links to motivational theories in an evaluation question. You need to look at a range of issues, including the business's structure, and then make a judgement as to how the leadership style affects the business. Autocratic can be the best approach if the business needs quick decisions.

Summary

After studying this topic, you should be able to:
- describe the different approaches to staffing, including the advantages and disadvantages of each approach
- describe the differences between dismissal and redundancy and employer–employee relationships
- describe the recruitment, selection and training process and the advantages and disadvantages of internal and external recruitment together with on-the-job and off-the-job training
- describe the different types of organisational structure, including centralised and decentralised structures
- discuss the advantages and disadvantages of different organisational structures
- describe the different theories of motivating employees, including their advantages and disadvantages to a business
- describe the autocratic, paternalistic, democratic and laissez-faire leadership approaches and their advantages and disadvantages

■ Entrepreneurs and leaders

Role of an entrepreneur

Creating and setting up a business

An entrepreneur is someone who takes a risk by starting a business. An entrepreneur creates and sets up a business, which involves having a business idea and the financial capital to make this idea a reality. The idea may come from observation that a key service is lacking locally, or may be the result of a scientific or technical study that leads to a new invention or innovation.

Further development is often done through a **business plan**, which is a forecast of business operations, including a cash flow forecast/statement of business objectives and a plan of staffing needs or marketing methods.

> **Knowledge check 23**
>
> Give a reason why Richard Branson is such a successful entrepreneur.

Running and expanding a business

Innovation within a business – intrapreneurship

Innovation within a business will come not only from the entrepreneur but also from employees and other people linked to the business.

An **intrapreneur** is someone within a business who takes risks in an effort to solve a given problem. This involves people within a business creating or discovering new business opportunities. This may lead to the creation of new parts of the business or even new businesses. In a business such as the Dyson company, intrapreneurship is encouraged by giving design engineers the time to develop their own product ideas.

Business plan Set of documents prepared by a firm's management to summarise its operational and financial objectives for the near future.

Innovation The process of translating an idea or invention into a good or service that creates value for which customers will pay.

Intrapreneur A person within a business who takes risks in an effort to seize an opportunity or solve a problem.

Barriers to entrepreneurship

Barriers to entrepreneurship include:

- financial barriers – the business cannot be started due to a lack of funding. This might be resolved by gaining backing from banks, from **crowd funding**, or from business angels (individuals who wish to invest money in a new business), government loans or grants
- competition barriers – already established businesses may put in place barriers to entering their market, such as city streets saturated with Starbucks and Costa cafés
- cultural barriers – in the past there was middle-class distain for those starting their own business. Today this is much less of a problem in Britain, where entrepreneurial skills are increasingly admired.

Knowledge check 25

How might a new entrepreneur be able to reduce the financial barriers of starting a business when seeking a loan from a bank?

Exam tip

Beware of assuming that enthusiasm is all it takes for an entrepreneur to succeed. The real keys are an insight into what the consumer *really* wants and a well-executed plan for delivering it in a distinctive, preferably unique, manner.

Anticipating risk and uncertainty in the business environment

Entrepreneurs must be able to anticipate risk and uncertainty in the business environment. This is done by looking at the size of the risk and comparing it to the possible rewards. By planning for the risks that impact on the business, such as a fall in customers' disposable income, the entrepreneur can reduce the level of uncertainty. Ultimately, the way to minimise risk in a business start-up is to have an idea so original and appealing that you can succeed even if various things go wrong. Most successful businesspeople have stories to tell about the things they mishandled in the early days. In effect, you need a large safety margin, so that problems seem more like pin pricks.

Entrepreneurial motives and characteristics

Entrepreneurial motives

Entrepreneurial motives are the reasons that drive a person or people to set up in business. These include financial motives such as making a profit or making the maximum profit available, known as **profit maximisation**.

Non-profit motives include:

- **satisficing** – the motive is to make sufficient profits to satisfy the entrepreneur but not necessarily the greatest profit possible
- **ethical stance** – starting a business with the intention of helping others, e.g. producing more comfortable wheelchairs for people with disabilities

Knowledge check 24

Explain the difference between an entrepreneur and an intrapreneur.

Crowd funding A method of raising capital by an online subscription from those interested in investing small sums in an interesting new business idea.

Exam tip

Make sure you don't confuse entrepreneurial motives and characteristics.

Knowledge check 26

Why might the ethical motives of Anita Roddick, founder of The Body Shop, have been a key factor in the success of her natural beauty product business?

- **social entrepreneurship** – the motive is to create a sustainable, profit-making business that also benefits the community, e.g. a second-hand bookshop
- **independence and home working** – the entrepreneur wants more freedom to work when and where they please, perhaps to fit around family or other commitments

Entrepreneurial characteristics

Entrepreneurial characteristics are personality traits and skills that an entrepreneur needs to have in order to start and run a successful business. The main characteristics are a risk-taking attitude, creativity, resilience (being able to cope with setbacks), self-confidence and determination.

Business objectives

An **objective** is the goal a business wants to achieve. This will depend on the stakeholders who are involved in the business. **Stakeholders** are defined as groups or individuals that are affected by and/or have an interest in the operations and objectives of the business.

The business objective may include:

- survival, to ensure the continuing existence of the business – this can apply to any business, but for a new business it is likely to be an objective due to the large amount of risk and uncertainty regarding its success
- profit maximisation, where producing a level of output of the product or service which generates the most profit for the business is important
- sales maximisation, where achieving the highest amount of sales revenue is most important (this does not make much business sense, but some companies in the past have worked at 'boosting sales to over £1 billion for the first time')
- market share, where the business focuses on capturing as many customers as possible, perhaps, like Facebook in its day, with a view to making profits later
- cost efficiency, where the business tries to reduce all its expenses to their lowest possible levels – this should ensure survival even in a toughly competitive market
- employee welfare, where the business tries to ensure the wellbeing and safety of its employees – this is likely to be one among several objectives
- customer satisfaction, where customers' needs and wants are met as much as possible (again, likely to be one among many objectives)
- social objectives, where the business tries to ensure it has the maximum positive impact on society and/or the environment

Forms of business

There are a number of ways a business can be set up.

A sole trader is a business with a single owner. It is the easiest method of starting a business and means the entrepreneur makes all the decisions and benefits exclusively from any profits. However, the owner is responsible personally for all risks and any losses. In other words, the owner has unlimited liability for any business debts.

Knowledge check 27

What might be a key entrepreneurial characteristic of tennis champion Andy Murray, which gains him sponsorship from sports clothing company Under Armour?

Exam tip

You will need to identify and evaluate the importance of specific characteristics from the stimulus material.

Knowledge check 28

After BP's oil disaster in the US in 2010, what objectives may now be of particular importance to its success?

Exam tip

Profit maximisation is often used as a focus for the 'evaluate' question. Remember, profits are needed to grow the business and pay back investors, so look at how established the business is to decide how important this objective is compared with others.

A **partnership** is a business owned by two or more people who share the decision making, risks and profits. The level of risk is lowered by sharing decision making and capital investment in the business between the partners. However, as decision making is shared, the business may develop in a way the entrepreneur disagrees with. Like a sole trader, a partnership has unlimited liability.

A **private limited company** is a business which is a separate legal entity to the entrepreneur and has limited liability. This means there will be shares in the business and the owner can only lose the capital they have invested in the business. Any further losses have to be borne by those the company owes money to. The shares are not traded publicly and the owner can choose whom to sell them to. Those holding shares are called shareholders. A private limited company reduces risks of financial losses to the entrepreneur as there is limited liability. However, the public are able to see various financial statements made by the business and the costs of setting up and running the company are much higher than the two forms mentioned above.

Franchising is an agreement where a business (the franchisor) sells the rights to other businesses (the franchisee) allowing them to sell the products or use the name for a percentage of the revenue generated. The business places the financial risks of setting up on the franchisee and the franchisor can grow very quickly as a result. However, franchisees can find they are working very hard but the franchisor is making most of the profit.

A **social enterprise** is a business whose aim is to reinvest profits in the business or community rather than being driven by the need to maximise profit for shareholders and owners.

Lifestyle businesses are set up and run by the entrepreneur with the aim of creating an enjoyable or prestigious position, leaving profit as a secondary consideration. An example is someone setting up a riding stables due to a love of horses.

Online businesses are set up to be run through the internet. They can adopt any of the approaches to setting up a business already discussed. They have low start-up costs and have access to a larger customer base than a physical business. However, unless the business has a unique product/service, competition is fierce in a usually saturated market.

Growth to a public limited company

A public limited company is defined as a business that is able to offer its shares to the public, normally through the stock market. There must be at least two shareholders and there are greater legal requirements to publish accounts than with a private limited company. As a company gets bigger it is likely that it will need access to a large amount of funds to ensure this growth continues. A public limited company can sell many shares and gain a significant amount of capital for growth. However, the original owner of the business will see their ownership diluted by the issuing of shares and will have less say over the way the business continues to operate.

Business choices

In order to manage risk and uncertainty, businesses will need to look at two factors.

| **Knowledge check 29** |
| Name one difference between a sole trader and a partnership. |

Exam tip

The key business issue is the difference between having and not having limited liability. In the UK, despite the advantages of limited liability, most firms are sole traders or partnerships and therefore have unlimited liability.

Exam tip

Make sure you know the differences between a private and a public limited company and can relate these to the stimulus material. Making a recommendation as to which is the best approach will impress the examiner.

Stock market A market where shares are bought and sold by the public.

Knowledge check 30

Why might John Lewis's success as a retailer be down to the fact that the only shareholders are staff who work for the business?

Opportunity cost measures the cost of any choice in terms of the next best alternative forgone. As the business has scarce resources, it needs to weigh up its choices when deciding on the way forward on a particular issue. This helps decide the least risky approach and reduces the level of uncertainty.

Trade-offs arise where having more of one thing potentially results in having less of another. The business will look at the possible trade-offs to try to ensure limited resources are used in the most effective way. For example, spending less money on market research may trade off with the less successful launch of a product, as the business does not have data about whether the product will meet customer needs.

It is important to remember that every pound spent in business has a trade-off because it is a pound that cannot be spent elsewhere.

Knowledge check 31

If a business selling hotdogs decides to spend £500 on advertising, what might be the opportunity cost of this course of action?

Exam tip

Make sure you know accurate definitions of trade-off and opportunity cost as students often confuse them. They are also a very good method of evaluating the two approaches in a 20-mark question and making a judgement as to the best way forward for the business.

Moving from entrepreneur to leader

There are difficulties in developing from an entrepreneur to a leader:

- Moving from control to delegation. As the business increases in size, the entrepreneur must learn to delegate authority and responsibility to employees in order to reduce stress levels and manage the significant increase in business issues that need to be resolved. This might mean moving away from an autocratic style of leadership.
- Moving to a more process-based method of decision making. As the business increases, so do the size of its risks. This means risks will need to be managed in a more scientific manner. An entrepreneur is likely to take a new product decision on the basis of hunch. A leader needs to make sure that senior staff understand why decisions are made and is therefore likely to use independent market researchers to find unbiased evidence.

Even entrepreneurs as successful as Alan Sugar and Steve Jobs have found it difficult to make the transition to leader.

Summary

After studying this topic, you should be able to:
- describe an entrepreneur in terms of their motives and characteristics and the barriers to entrepreneurship, including how risk and uncertainty can be anticipated
- explain a business plan and its advantages and disadvantages to starting a business
- explain the importance of innovation and intrapreneurship in running and expanding a business
- explain how an entrepreneur can move to becoming a leader
- describe different business objectives and the different forms of business
- discuss the advantages and disadvantages of the different forms of business
- describe what is meant by opportunity cost and trade-off

Questions & Answers

Exam questions and answers

The questions and answers in this section of the book follow a similar structure to the exams. There are extracts from business situations, data and a selection of all the different types of questions you will be asked to answer in either the AS exam or the A-level exam. Above each question it indicates in which exam this type of question will be found. Please note that the extracts have been kept to a minimum so as to allow for a greater range of questions and answers. This means that AS and A-level questions have been related to the same extracts, which will not be the case in the actual exams.

For the AS exam there are six 2-mark questions and three 20-mark questions. For the AS/A-level exams there are three 4-mark questions and three 8-mark questions. For the A-level exam there are two 12-mark questions. All 20-mark questions cover both Theme 1 and Theme 2, as in the actual AS exam. However, please note the content of Theme 2 is covered in Student Guide 2, not in this guide.

All questions give a Student A and a Student B answer. One will be a lower-grade answer and the other will be an upper-grade answer.

Exam structure

A-level Business consists of three two-hour exams. Paper 1 covers half the course: Theme 1 from AS plus Theme 4 from the second year of study. So the subject content for Paper 1 is 'Marketing and people'. Paper 2 covers the other half of the subject content, Themes 2 and 3. Paper 3 covers all subject content, including Theme 1, the subject of this book. Each exam consists of Sections A and B, with all questions compulsory. Sections A and B will each have one question broken down into parts based on data and extracts provided in the exam. In Papers 1 and 2 the questions carry 4, 10, 12 or 20 marks. For Paper 3 the questions carry 8, 10, 12 or 20 marks. In the case of Paper 3, the business context for the questions will be issued in the November prior to the exam. Section A questions will be based on the market as a whole (for instance, the UK motor industry) and Section B questions on a specific company, for example Jaguar Land Rover. The total score for each paper is 100 marks.

AS Business consists of two exams. Paper 1 is based on 'Marketing and people' (Theme 1, i.e. the content of this book), though the final, 20-mark question will relate a concept from Theme 1 to one from Theme 2. The exam lasts for 1 hour 30 minutes and consists of Sections A, B and C, with all questions compulsory. Sections A and B each have extracts based on real businesses, with questions carrying the following mark 'tariffs': 2 × 2 marks, 2 × 4 marks, 1 × 8 marks and 1 × 10 marks. Section C is a single 20-mark question requiring you to make connections between Themes 1 and 2 in your answers. The 20-mark question requires you to analyse two different options facing a business, then make a fully evaluated recommendation about which should be chosen. The total score for this paper is 80 marks, giving 10 minutes of reading time and then a minute per mark. Paper 2, 'Managing business activities', adopts exactly the same structure, marks and exam time, and is the focus of Student Guide 2.

Exam skills

For AS Business Papers 1 and 2, 2-mark questions require knowledge of business terms. All other questions have the same skills requirements as the A-level.

Questions with 4 marks require knowledge of business terms, specific application of the business term from the stimulus material, and an advantage and/or disadvantage of the business term related to the stimulus material. These questions may also ask you to calculate answers using formulas you have learnt and data in the stimulus material. The examiner will mark this type of question 'from the bottom up'. This means each mark is earned individually, so you get marks for an advantage, for example, even though you have not provided any context from the stimulus material. Context is anything specifically related to the business in the extract. Your discussion must relate back to the question.

At AS, 8-mark questions have a specific exam technique. Each 8-marker asks you to 'assess two factors/reasons' and allocates 4 marks to each factor. This means that the only way to get 8/8 is as follows: for each answer you need to generate 1 mark for each of the following assessment objectives: knowledge, application, analysis and evaluation. Therefore you get full marks in the following way:

$$(1 + 1 + 1 + 1) + (1 + 1 + 1 + 1) = 8$$

The only plausible way to achieve this is to write four sentences for each part: one sentence setting out knowledge, one applying it to the context provided, one building up your answer using the theory of the subject and one giving judgement (evaluation).

Questions with 8, 10, 12 and 20 marks require evaluation of the business term using specific evidence from the extract. The safest way to do this is to provide a strong, two-sided argument. It also suggests making judgements about the business and the key terms discussed, together with proposing solutions to business problems based on the stimulus material and your business knowledge. The examiner will mark these types of question from a 'best fit' point of view. This means examiners will give you marks for the highest level of response you show in your answer. For the 8-mark question to obtain full marks, two reasons/factors need to be discussed with a two-sided argument, though the level of detail expected will be less than for the 10-, 12- or 20-mark questions. It is worth emphasising the statements at the top level (Level 4) of Edexcel's mark schemes:

'Accurate and thorough knowledge and understanding, supported throughout by relevant and effective use of the business behaviour/context.

Uses well-developed and logical, coherent chains of reasoning, showing a range of cause and/or effect(s).

Arguments are fully developed.

Quantitative and/or qualitative information is/are used well to support judgements. A full awareness of the validity and significance of competing arguments/factors, leading to balanced comparisons, judgements and an effective conclusion that proposes a solution and/or recommendations.'

Technique when evaluating 20-mark questions

As this is the most challenging essay to write on the paper, the examiner is looking for detailed evaluation of two approaches in Theme 1 against an issue from Theme 2. The judgement or conclusion must include some reference to MOPS:

■ **Market:** characteristics of the market in which the business operates. How does this influence your conclusion? For example, Apple is in the smartphone market, which is dynamic and fast changing, and it therefore has to spend a lot of money on research and development to ensure it keeps its competitive advantage.

■ **Objectives:** how do the business's objectives align to the situation in which it finds itself? What are the objectives of the business? How does this influence your conclusion? For example, Apple's objective might be increasing market share, so being the most novel product regardless of the cost may be of greatest importance.

■ **Product:** what products or services does the business sell? How might this influence your thinking? For example, Apple may bring out a cheaper iPhone in garish colours to capture more market share.

■ **Situation:** what is the current situation the business finds itself in? Does this affect your conclusion? For example, with sales of smartphones peaking, Apple needs to find an extension strategy, such as selling to other global markets, for instance India, to maintain/improve market share, hence the need for a cheaper phone.

You need to read the extract and the question and use the most appropriate element of MOPS in this context to consider the wider issues affecting the business that will influence the key issues in the question.

1 The UK milk market

Extract A

The milk market is worth £2 billion per year in the UK (June 2011), with milk being sold in cheap, clear plastic containers in litres at supermarkets, such as Tesco or Aldi, typically having little attention paid to the packaging other than the name and type of milk. 1 litre of milk typically sells for £0.75 across most shops and has a shelf life of 2–3 days.

Cravendale is a brand of milk launched by UK company Arla in 2004. It uses a special type of filtering to remove more impurities from the milk than ordinary milk. Together with white plastic bottles and labels that stand out, the milk has a shelf life of up to 3 weeks. Cravendale has a sophisticated marketing campaign using television adverts and social media to raise awareness of the product, spending £5m on advertising per year. Cravendale is sold in supermarkets at a premium price of £1.15 per litre. Arla posted profits of £8.3m in 2012.

Tesco has now launched its own brand of filtered milk at the lower price of £0.95 per litre.

Dynamic market

AS question

What is meant by a dynamic market? (2 marks)

🅮 The 'what is meant by' command words mean you need to define the business term in the question and either develop this or give an example.

Understanding: of what is meant by a dynamic market (AO1). This is worth up to 2 marks and can include an enhanced definition or a basic definition and an example of a dynamic market.

Accurate definitions are critical for marks.

> **Student A**
>
> A dynamic market that is constantly changing as it can grow, change and decline very quickly. ⓐ For example Apple. ⓑ

🅮 **1/2 marks awarded** ⓐ The student has recalled the precise and accurate definition of a dynamic market to gain an easy 1 AO1 mark. ⓑ Even though the student used the name 'Apple', there needs to be a brief explanation as to how this relates to a dynamic market, so no mark is awarded.

> **Student B**
>
> A dynamic market that is constantly changing as it can grow, change and decline very quickly. ⓐ
>
> The market for smartphones. ⓑ

🅮 **2/2 marks awarded** ⓐ The student has recalled the precise and accurate definition of a dynamic market to gain an easy AO1 mark. ⓑ The example of smartphones is self-explanatory (it is a dynamic market whereas Apple is a company, not a market).

This is a very straightforward question and you should be able to score 2 out of the 2 marks allocated. For Student A to score only 1 mark (grade U) shows a lack of preparation and understanding of the skills needed to answer the question. Student B scores 2 marks (Grade A) simply by giving a relevant example.

When revising, make sure you prepare an accurate definition with a related example so you are ready for such 2-mark questions.

Mass and niche markets

AS/A-level question

Explain, using Extract A, how Cravendale could be disadvantaged by Tesco introducing its own niche milk product in the market. (4 marks)

(e) The 'explain' command word means you need a definition with how this links to the stimulus material, justifying your answer.

Understanding: of what is meant by a niche market (AO1). This is worth 1 mark.

Application: for contextualised examples of how Cravendale could be disadvantaged (AO2). This is worth up to 2 marks.

Analysis: developing a reason/cause/consequence of a disadvantage of a niche market (AO3). This is worth up to 1 mark.

Student A

A niche market is a larger part of a mass market. a Cravendale milk is a niche market product. b

One disadvantage of Cravendale operating in a niche market is with fewer potential customers compared with a mass market product, costs in making the product will be higher. c

---

(e) **1/4 marks awarded** a The student has not recalled the precise and accurate definition of a niche market to gain an easy mark. b Even though the student uses the name 'Cravendale' and relates it to niche market, the answer still needs to give more specific information from the stimulus material as to why this is the case here to gain the application AO2 mark. c The student gives an accurate disadvantage for a business that operates in a niche market and scores 1 AO3 mark. However, even though they have used the unique name of the business 'Cravendale' in their answer, this still does not get another mark for application to the stimulus material. Simply quoting from the stimulus material is not enough to gain application marks. You must relate the information you use from the stimulus material to the theory on niche markets. The student should go on and give further development of their disadvantage but fails to do this.

Student B

A niche market is the smaller section of a larger market on which a product or service is focused by a business. The products tend to have unique characteristics. a

One disadvantage of Cravendale operating in a niche market is with fewer potential customers compared to a mass market product, costs in making the product will be higher, hence the higher sale price of £1.15 per litre. b As a consequence, Tesco selling a similar product at a cheaper price to customers of £0.95 per litre will mean Cravendale will lose customers from what is already a potentially small market. c

---

(e) **4/4 marks awarded** a The student has recalled the precise and accurate definition of a niche market to gain an easy 1 mark and AO1. b The student gives an accurate disadvantage for a business that operates in a niche market, with relevant context from the stimulus material, and scores 1 mark for AO2 and 1 for AO3. c The student develops this point further to show the potential impact on Cravendale of another competitor entering the niche market, gaining another application mark.

This is a quite straightforward question and you should be able to score at least 3 of the 4 marks allocated. For Student A to score only 1 mark (grade U) shows a lack of preparation and understanding of the skills needed to answer the question. Student B scores 4 marks (Grade A) simply because he/she has learnt some straightforward business and clearly developed their analysis of niche markets in the specific context of the question, using the stimulus material to good effect.

Extract B

Arla Foods has decided to try to reduce the costs of Cravendale milk to customers by moving production to Latvia. The mark-up per 1 litre bottle of milk is 10.5%. The filtering process allows the milk to stay fresh for up to 45 days unopened at 7°C while it is transported to the UK for sale in supermarkets.

Costs of manufacturing Cravendale milk in Latvia

Component costs	Euros (€)
Filtered milk cost per litre	0.50
1 litre plastic bottle	0.10
Label cost per bottle	0.05
Transport costs	0.30

Market orientation

AS/A-level question

Assess the possible benefits to Cravendale milk of being market orientated. (10 marks)

ⓔ The 'assess' command word means students need to supply an answer with advantages and disadvantages of the business concept. The question is asking for problems for a business with market orientation, with the highest skill evidenced being evaluation. The relevant extract provided by the examiner should be referred to when answering the question.

Level 1: this is for giving a benefit of a business being market orientated or maybe a problem or a definition of market orientated. The student will not have used application correctly. There will be no advantages/disadvantages, or they will be poorly discussed. This is worth a maximum of 2 marks, for instance by giving an example of being market orientated.

Level 2: this is for giving an implication of the business being market orientated – for example, what does this mean to the business in the context of the situation? The student will have used application correctly. There will be an advantage or disadvantage. This is worth up to 2 marks.

Level 3: this is for giving a reason why market orientation will be a benefit or drawback for the business. The student will have used application correctly. There will be an advantage and a disadvantage which have used application correctly. This is worth up to 2 marks.

Level 4: this is for giving a reason why market orientation may be a risk for the business. The student will have used application correctly. There will be an advantage and a disadvantage which have used application correctly. The advantages and disadvantages will link together and the evaluation will be detailed. A judgement or recommendation is made and explained. This is worth up to 4 marks.

Questions & Answers

To gain good marks, give at least one advantage and one disadvantage, saying why this is the most important issue related to the stimulus material.

> **Student A**
>
> Market orientation is where a business chooses to provide a product or service to meet the needs of customers. ⓐ Cravendale seeks to meet customer needs by selling milk. ⓑ One advantage of Cravendale milk using market orientation is they try and closely match customer expectations. ⓒ A disadvantage of market orientation is that doing market research is expensive, for example sending surveys to customers is time consuming and looking at the results costs money. ⓓ I would recommend Cravendale not being market orientated as it costs too much money compared to being product orientated, ⓔ where a business chooses to ignore their customer's needs and focus only on efficiently building a quality good or service. ⓕ

ⓔ **4/10 marks awarded** ⓐ The student has recalled a sufficiently precise and accurate definition of market orientation to gain 1 mark and Level 1. ⓑ Even though the student uses the name 'Cravendale' and relates it to selling milk, the student does not relate this to market orientation so no mark is awarded. ⓒ The advantage is not well explained so is regarded as superficial and can be awarded only 2 marks and Level 2 (3 so far). ⓓ The student's example of a disadvantage, that market orientation is very expensive, is a general statement that can be applied to many business concepts. It is also good technique to use the words from the question in the answer, so rather than use 'advantage', the word 'benefit' would show better understanding of the question. However, this point has been developed to make a general drawback related to market orientations, so gains 1 mark and Level 4 (4 so far). ⓔ The attempt to form a judgement is based on pure assumptions and not on an accurate development of the student's earlier answer so gains no further mark or level. ⓕ This is simply a definition of product orientation rather than a development of the student's judgement, gaining no marks or level.

If you can substitute another business (for example, Cadbury) in your answer and it still makes sense, your answer will not gain any marks for applying it to a business context as it is too generic. You need to make your answer more unique to the stimulus material as it shows the examiner how this relates back to answering the question.

> **Student B**
>
> Market orientation is where a business chooses to provide a product or service to meet the customers' desires, wants or needs. ⓐ Cravendale seeks to meet customer needs by selling milk that has a three-week shelf life. ⓑ One advantage of Cravendale milk using market orientation is that the product will closely match customer expectations. ⓒ As a consequence, Cravendale have differentiated their product from regular milk by making it last longer, meaning they can charge a higher price of £1.15 per litre compared to normal milk of £0.75 per litre. ⓓ

However, a disadvantage of market orientation is that a lot of time needs to be spent on market research to ensure customers' needs are always reflected in the development of the product. e Tesco introducing lower priced filtered milk at £0.95 per litre appears to suggest that Cravendale have not done enough market research on the correct price of their product, potentially resulting in lower profits. f Cravendale need to make sure that if they are to use market orientation they must invest more time and money in market research such as focus groups to ask customers about issues such as the correct selling price of the product. g This way they can anticipate customer needs and drop the price of their filtered milk before competitors such as Tesco gain this competitive advantage, ensuring profits of £8.3m are maintained in future years. h

e **10/10 marks awarded** a The student has recalled a precise and accurate definition of market orientation to gain 1 mark and Level 1. b There is clear use of the stimulus material to show how market orientation is reflected in Cravendale's product, gaining 2 marks and Level 2 (3 so far). c The advantage lacks development so far, so gains 1 mark and Level 2 (4 so far). d 'As a consequence' shows a further development of this point and cause and effect for Cravendale, i.e. the ability to charge higher prices, showing clear analysis and gaining 2 marks and Level 3 (6 so far). e A disadvantage is discussed which is generic but gains 1 mark and Level 4 (7 so far). f The student develops the disadvantage critically with specific information from the stimulus material, so gains 1 mark and Level 4 (8 so far). g The student now makes a developed judgement about what Cravendale might do to limit the potential disadvantage of market orientation, gaining 1 mark and Level 4 (9 so far). h This judgement is developed and supported, linking back to the stimulus material, gaining 1 mark and Level 4 (10 in total).

Student A needs to use more context to develop their answer and makes assumptions rather than basing their answer on logical interpretation of the stimulus material, gaining only an E grade. Student B uses the stimulus material well to make a logical evaluation and judgement of Cravendale milk and the market orientation. They use context very well to gain an A-grade answer.

Income elasticity of demand

A-level question

Assess the likely impact of an increase in consumer incomes on the demand for milk such as that made by Arla.

(12 marks)

e The 'assess' command word means students need to supply an extract-based answer with advantages and disadvantages of the business concept. They also need to make a judgement about the business term in the context of the stimulus material and include other relevant business theories. Extract B can be used to provide application, but the words 'such as' in the question mean the student can base their application on any similar business.

Questions & Answers

Level 1: this is for giving a likely impact on demand for Arla milk or a definition of demand or income elasticity of demand. The student will not have used application correctly. There will be no advantages/disadvantages, or they will be poorly discussed. This is worth a maximum of 2 marks, for example defining waste.

Level 2: this is for giving a likely impact on demand for Arla milk or a definition of demand or income elasticity of demand. The student will have used application correctly. There will be an advantage or a disadvantage. This is worth up to 2 marks.

Level 3: this is for giving a likely impact on demand for Arla milk or a definition of demand or income elasticity of demand. The student will have used application correctly. There will be an advantage and a disadvantage which have used application correctly. This is worth up to 4 marks.

Level 4: this is for giving a likely impact on demand for Arla milk or a definition of demand or income elasticity of demand. The student will have used application correctly. There will be an advantage and a disadvantage which have used application correctly. The advantages and disadvantages will link together and the evaluation will be coherent and wide ranging. A judgement will be made about the business term in the context of the question. This is worth up to 4 marks.

Student A

Demand is the amount of a good or service which a customer buys at a given price. a Demand for Cravendale milk has been high as they have made a profit of £8.3m in 2012. b One advantage of an increase in consumer incomes is that they will buy more of the product. c This means the demand curve will move to the right and demand will go up, resulting in consumers buying more of Arla's filtered milk. d If consumer incomes go down then the demand curve will shift to the left and demand will go down. e Cravendale milk will make more money if consumer incomes increase. f

e **5/12 marks awarded** a The student has recalled a definition of demand that is sufficient to be awarded 1 mark and Level 1. b The student has linked the context of Arla's profit in 2012 to demand, but this is a weak assumption and could be due to many other factors – gains 1 mark and Level 1 (2 so far). c The advantage is correctly explained in the context of demand and is regarded as analysis. However, as the student hasn't provided any context relevant to the stimulus material, the answer is generic and gains 2 marks and Level 2 (4 so far). d The student attempts to develop the advantage with some context and gains 1 mark and Level 2 (5 so far). e The student is not directly answering the question so gains no further mark or level. f This is simply an assumption, with no development as to why Arla may make more profit, and the use of 'Cravendale' is not sufficient to be classed as context as it is not used to answer the question, so no marks or level awarded.

Student B

Income elasticity of demand measures the responsiveness of demand after a change in customer income. a One advantage of an increase in consumer incomes is that according to the theory of income elasticity of demand, they will buy more Cravendale milk. b This is because Arla's milk is likely to be regarded as a luxury rather than a necessity product as it is more expensive to buy. c This means it is income elastic and therefore customers who normally buy normal milk will switch to Cravendale when they have more disposable income. d A likely impact on Arla is that they increase their profits from their 2012 levels of £8.3m. e

However, the increase in Arla's product sales depends on the number of other competitors also operating in the niche market for milk. f As the extract states, Tesco also have entered the filtered milk market with a similar product to Cravendale but at a lower price of £0.95 per litre. g As a consequence this could be regarded as penetration pricing by Tesco, which would have the negative impact on Arla of attracting customers away from their product to Tesco's. h This would mean Arla's profits would not increase as significantly as if they were the only producer of filtered milk. Arla should reduce their price so they can make more profit and gain market share from Tesco. i

e **9/12 marks awarded** a The student has recalled a very precise and accurate definition of income elasticity of demand to gain 1 mark and Level 1. b The student has given an advantage of income elasticity of demand but needs further development for a mark. c The advantage is explained to suggest that, as Cravendale is a luxury, demand will increase as income increases, and as this includes sufficient context from the stimulus material it is enough to give 3 marks and Level 2 (4 so far). d The student further develops the impact of income rising, relating Cravendale to income elasticity for 1 mark and Level 3 (5 so far). e The student relates the developed point to a likely impact on Arla, a rise in profits, using the stimulus material figures to good effect, and gains 2 marks and Level 3 (7 so far). f A potential negative impact regarding the actions of other competitors in the market is introduced but needs further development, so gains no further marks. g The student correctly links Tesco as a competitor using the context, but the actual effect is not yet mentioned so no further marks are awarded. h The consequence correctly shows the negative impact on Arla, using a potential pricing strategy Tesco may be using with their product, based on information from the stimulus material – this gains 2 marks and Level 4 (9 so far). i The student attempts to make a judgement as to what Arla might do to reduce the impact of Tesco on milk sales, but the point is not developed so gains no further marks.

Student A fails to use the stimulus material to enhance their answer and the advantage they give is very general so fails to gain marks for analysis. Note that the student's fundamental weakness in this answer is poor application to context. This could have been a much improved answer if the student had just used the stimulus material better in their answer, so gains only a D grade. Student B uses the stimulus material well to give a benefit and risk in context, but rather drifts away from the question in the second part of the answer. The answer also lacks a developed judgement and recommendation as to what Arla should do, so gains low-level evaluation but still a B grade.

Product portfolio and business objectives

Extract C

Arla is a global farmer-owned co-operative.

The United Kingdom is currently the biggest market, with revenue of almost £1.4 billion in 2012.

Arla aims to become the largest dairy company in the United Kingdom and have a wide range of fresh dairy products, including UHT milk and, as a new feature, cheese production. Arla's aim is for revenue to increase by nearly £0.5 billion annually.

AS only

Arla is considering how its objective of maximising market share could be achieved using either the product life cycle or the Boston Matrix for managing its products.

Evaluate these two options and recommend which is the most suitable for a business such as Arla.

(20 marks)

ⓔ The 'evaluate' command word means you need to review the pros and cons of the business term using stimulus material. Weigh up strengths and weaknesses of arguments and then support a specific judgement, forming a recommendation and a conclusion. Extract C can be used to provide application, but the words 'such as' in the question mean the student can base their application on any similar business.

Level 1: this is for giving a reason, a definition or some knowledge of the product life cycle or Boston Matrix method of managing products. The student will not have used application correctly. There will be no advantages/disadvantages or they will be poorly discussed. This is worth a maximum of 4 marks, for example by giving detailed definitions of the product life cycle and the Boston Matrix.

Level 2: this is for giving a reason, a definition or some knowledge of the product life cycle or Boston Matrix method of managing products. The student will have used application correctly. There will be an advantage or disadvantage of the product life cycle and/or the Boston Matrix, but they will be poorly developed. This is worth up to 4 marks.

Level 3: this is for giving a reason, a definition or some knowledge of the product life cycle or Boston Matrix method of managing products. The student will have used application correctly. There will be an advantage and a disadvantage which have used application correctly for the product life cycle or the Boston Matrix. There may be evaluation of the product life cycle or the Boston Matrix and its ability to be cost efficient, but it is poorly developed. This is worth up to 6 marks.

Level 4: this is for giving a reason, a definition or some knowledge of the product life cycle or Boston Matrix method of managing products. The student will have used application correctly. There will be an advantage and disadvantage, which have used application correctly for the product portfolio or the Boston Matrix. The advantages and disadvantages of the product portfolio and/or the Boston Matrix will link together coherently and the evaluation will be detailed and wide ranging. A judgement and recommendation will be made about the best approach for the business to achieve the objective of maximising market share, with a conclusion. This is worth up to 6 marks.

Student A

Product portfolio is defined as the term given to a business which has a number of products. a Product portfolio links to the Boston Matrix, which is a method of measuring the success of a business's products compared to others in the market. b The business can identify which products are doing well, called stars, and those products which are not doing well, called dogs. c

In Arla's case their Boston Matrix is important as they can decide whether their current range of products is doing well compared to competitors' products. d The advantage of using the Boston Matrix to analyse Arla's product is they can identify which products need money spent on them in terms of product development. e These would be called a problem child and this further product development would allow Arla to gain a competitive advantage over other products that the rising star is competing against. f This would mean they can improve their product portfolio and make greater profit by taking market share off other businesses in the market. g

The Boston Matrix is also important as it lets Arla identify products which are called dogs. h Any of Arla's products in this category have low market share and are no longer competitive in the market so should be phased out of their product portfolio. i Arla need to get rid of these products from their portfolio as they will not make them any profit. j

In conclusion, I think Arla should spend money on problem child products as this would make them more profit. k They should get rid of any dogs from their product portfolio as these products only lose them money and reduce their profit overall. l

e **8/20 marks awarded** a The student has recalled a definition of product portfolio rather than the product life cycle so gains no marks. b The student has defined the Boston Matrix accurately and related this to assessing a product portfolio, which is worth 1 mark and Level 1. c The student develops this explanation of the Boston Matrix in detail, but the content so far is simply knowledge so is worth only 2 more marks and Level 1 (3 so far). d The student attempts to discuss the benefit of using a Boston Matrix but it lacks any context from the stimulus material or development so will gain 2 marks and Level 2 (5 so far). e The student develops the benefit of the Boston Matrix but without context that shows it is understood how this applies to Arla so gains 2 marks and Level 2 (7 so far). As Arla is in the question, this would not be classed as context, so no further mark or level is awarded for this attempt at context. f This is further development of the benefit of using the product portfolio, with no development as to why Arla may benefit from its use, so no further marks or level can be awarded. g Again, another developed point, but as it is only theory and not applied to the stimulus material, no further level or marks can be awarded. h The student attempts to make a judgement and recommendation about products classed as dogs. i This is further developed to show a consequence of not getting rid of these types of products but has no context and the development is weak, so gains 1 mark and Level 2 (8 so far). j–l The student attempts a recommendation and conclusion, but as these are just duplicating what has already been discussed and have no context, they gain no further marks or level.

Questions & Answers

The Boston Matrix allows the business to analyse their products' performance in comparison to other competitors in the market. ☐ This applies to Arla as Extracts A–C show that not only do they have Cravendale milk as a product but also many other dairy products such as 'UHT' and the 'new feature' product of cheese. ☐

Business objectives are the goals the business wants to achieve and include Arla's aim of gaining the largest share of customers in the milk and dairy market. ☐ As Arla's biggest market is the UK, with £1.4bn of revenue, it is important for Arla to ensure its range of products in its product portfolio meet its current and future business objectives. ☐ The Boston Matrix can identify which products require the most investment and which don't, ☐ for example Cravendale milk might be described as a cash cow as it may have high market share as it is a niche market product with few current competitors. ☐ As a consequence, this would be a product that has little further growth due to the relatively small nature of a niche market product so it has already satisfied Arla's objective of capturing market share, having contributed to £1.4bn annual revenue. ☐ Arla would therefore need to simply maintain the high market share of Cravendale through marketing and promotion but do not have to spend any money on product design or development meeting their objective. ☐

However, Extract A states that Tesco are entering the market with their own filtered milk at a lower price per litre than Cravendale. ☐ The Boston Matrix would help identify this competitor, though it is not likely to do so until Tesco have entered the market, which means Arla could not have taken steps to protect their market share objective straight away. ☐ This shows a problem with using the Boston Matrix to help manage product portfolio in that it only measures competitors that are already known about, so Arla could not use this method to react quickly to changes in a dynamic market, in protecting their market share. ☐

The product life cycle describes the stages a product goes through from when it was first thought of until it finally is removed from the market. ☐ Arla's Cravendale may be described as reaching maturity if they have looked at past sales figures and find they are no longer increasing, which means the product life cycle helps them to identify when such a product appears to have reached its maximum potential. ☐ As a consequence, the product life cycle would allow Arla to decide on whether to invest in an extension strategy, such as moving production to Latvia, as they have done, to reduce costs and maintain market share of the product by lowering the selling price so they can still maintain market share. ☐ Or Arla may wish to introduce a new product, such as the new cheese range, which will be at the introduction stage of the product life cycle. ☐

However, unlike the Boston Matrix, Arla will only have records of sales to gauge the product life cycle so the problem for Arla is they will not know who their competitors are or the potential size of the dairy market without other information such as secondary market research such as Mintel reports. ☐ Without this data Arla would simply be guessing as to whether Cravendale milk's market share had reached their objective maximum market share and as a consequence the product may still be in the growth stage, as perhaps shown by new competitors entering the market such as Tesco. g

Due to the weaknesses of the Boston Matrix and the product life cycle, the best approach for Arla to maximise market share is to combine both methods of analysing their product portfolio. r In order to do this successfully they will need to gather primary and secondary market research in a way that allows them to understand the size of the potential market, so they can accurately assess what stage their products are at, and also react quickly enough to identify new competitors who are likely to steal market share. s This will help Arla strike the right balance in making the correct decisions in terms of investment and promotional spending for each product and maximise their revenue and market share. t

e 20/20 marks awarded a The student has recalled a definition of product portfolio which is precise enough to be awarded 1 mark and AO1. b The student has linked the context of Arla's different products, specifically quoting from the stimulus material, and attempted to relate this back to answering the question, so gains 2 more marks and Level 1 (3 marks so far). c The student correctly gives examples of business objectives as the product portfolio should be discussed in the context of these issues. However, as there is no specific context or consequence the answer is awarded no further marks or level. d The student relates Arla's business objectives to both the product portfolio and the context, meaning a further 2 marks and Level 2 (5 marks so far). e The student gives one reason why the Boston Matrix is important to analysing Arla's products. f This is then put into context, with the student making a logical statement about Cravendale and it being a cash cow, giving a further 2 marks and Level 2 (7 marks so far). g This point is then developed to show how the Boston Matrix can identify products that have contributed to market share, in context, and the consequence of this in terms of Arla's objective of gaining market share with some development, meaning another 2 marks and Level 3 (9 marks so far). h The student makes further development of the benefit of the Boston Matrix to Arla, critical to achieving its market share objective, which means another mark and Level 3 (10 marks so far). i The student then starts to give a problem with using the Boston Matrix in relation to Tesco's filtered milk, but it is not developed to answer the question so is worth no further mark or level. j The student shows a problem in using the Boston Matrix. k The student relates the problems with the Boston Matrix to its ability to be used as a mechanism for reacting to a dynamic market, gaining 2 marks and Level 3 (12 marks so far). l The student defines product life cycle but gains no further mark as this is simply knowledge, with maximum credit already given for this element of the answer. m The student uses specific context to show a benefit of using the product life cycle, but as it is not related back to the market share object, it gains no further mark. n This point is further developed and related to the extracts and the market share objective to gain 2 marks and Level 3 (14 so far). o The student gives an alternative use of the product life cycle, comparing different products and stages in context and gaining 1 mark and Level 4 (15 marks so far). d The student then highlights a problem with using the product life cycle in that it does not by itself show the business where it is in terms of market share compared with current market share. e The student develops this point with very good use of MOPS and the extract, gaining 2 marks and Level 4 (17 so far). f The student then makes a recommendation about the use of the Boston Matrix and the product life cycle in the context of helping achieve market share for 1 mark and Level 4 (18 so far). g The student makes a judgement and conclusion as to how to the proposed strategy may help achieve and monitor the objective of increased market share for 1 mark and Level 4 (19 so far). h The student gives a conclusion on the benefits of the proposed strategy for a further mark and Level 4 (20 marks in total).

Student A analyses the Boston Matrix but has not used the stimulus material in context. The student has not evaluated the use of the Boston Matrix in the context of achieving maximum market share and in comparison with the product life cycle. The student needed to understand the question and its requirements to a greater extent to gain better marks and as a result achieves only a grade D. Student B presents an outstanding answer showing a balanced and valid range of arguments, with excellent use of the stimulus material and wider business knowledge, including the use of MOPS to form a judgement and recommendation, thus gaining an A.

The main issue with this response is one of timing. Only write sufficient to gain the 20 marks and make sure you spend only 20 minutes on any answer for AS and 24 minutes for A-level. Practice in timed conditions is the best way to gauge your ability to answer this type of question.

2 Magmatic suitcases

Extract A

Rob Law, an entrepreneur, presented his idea for a ride-on suitcase for toddlers to *Dragons' Den*, the famous television programme, but was rejected. Ten years later his business had sold 3m 'Trunkis' and they have become the travel case for middle-class parents around the world.

Law has now invented a suitcase for teenagers called the 'Jurni', which is small enough to be hand luggage but strong enough for someone to sit on.

The case, with a retail price of £80, has skateboard wheels and doubles as a bedside cabinet, with special waterproof storage for electronic gadgets. Law says he is marketing the product at so-called 'lazy' teens. 'Thirteen-year-olds don't want things that look like toys, they want adult products. But they've also got specific needs,' he says.

Law puts his success down to determination, persistence and a need to be creative.

Extract B

The Trunki and the Jurni are both developed and sold through Rob Law's company, Magmatic Ltd, of which he has 50% shares and which is valued at £13m. The company has had to spend over £1m fighting court battles over its rights to its innovative case designs and copies being made in the UK and abroad. This has contributed to company losses of £1.4m in 2015.

Magmatic has completed extensive market research looking at the optimum selling price of the Jurni in the UK market for the first year of sale with the results, shown in the table.

Price (£)	Quantity
50	6,000
60	5,000
70	4,000
80	3,000
90	2,000

Magmatic has traditionally sold products through retailers such as Marks and Spencer but the latest market research suggests selling directly through its own retail outlets could help boost sales dramatically, linking closely with its successful Trunki online shop.

Extract C

This year Magmatic is on track to sell 2m of its suitcases worldwide. Its products are now stocked in more than 2,500 stores across the UK, as well as in 97 countries. Trunki views China, Japan, Germany, France and India as particular growth markets.

Source: Business Zone, www.businesszone.co.uk/delete/idiot-box/start-up-stories-proving-the-dragons-wrong-rob-law-at-trunki

Entrepreneur and innovation

AS-only question

What is meant by an entrepreneur? (2 marks)

e The 'what is meant by' command words mean you need a definition of the business term in the question and either this can be developed or an example can be given.

Understanding: of what is meant by an entrepreneur (AO1). This is worth up to 2 marks and can include an enhanced definition or a basic definition and an example of an entrepreneur as long as it relates back to the definition, including use of the stimulus material.

Accurate definitions are critical for marks.

Student A

An example of an entrepreneur is Richard Branson. **a** Another example from Extract A is Rob Law. **b**

@ **0/2 marks awarded** a The student has simply given an example of a well-known entrepreneur but shows no knowledge of the term, so no mark is awarded. b The example of an entrepreneur from the stimulus material again shows no understanding of the term, so no marks.

> **Student B**
>
> An entrepreneur is someone who takes a risk by starting a business. a Rob Law is an entrepreneur. b

@ **1/2 marks awarded** a The student has recalled the definition of an entrepreneur to gain an easy mark and AO1. b The example of Rob Law does not show knowledge of what makes him an entrepreneur, so no mark is awarded.

This is a straightforward question and you should be able to score 2 out of the 2 marks allocated. For Student A to score 0 marks (grade U) shows a lack of preparation and understanding of the skills needed to answer the question. Student B shows a lack of understanding of what the question requires for a second mark and gains a grade D.

What is meant by innovation? (2 marks)

> **Student A**
>
> An example of innovation is the new Jurni suitcase. a

@ **0/2 marks awarded** a The example of innovation from the stimulus material shows no understanding of the term, so no marks.

> **Student B**
>
> Innovation is bringing a new idea into practice, either as a new product hits the market or as a new process (such as a new way of manufacturing). a

@ **2/2 marks awarded** a This is a detailed explanation of innovation, even though the student has kept the answer quite brief.

This is a straightforward question and you should be able to score both marks allocated. For Student A to score 0 marks (grade U) shows a lack of preparation and understanding of the skills needed to answer the question.

Total revenue

AS/A-level question

Using the data from Extract B, calculate the total revenue for the Jurni suitcase. (4 marks)

@ The 'using' and 'calculate' command words mean your answer must complete a calculation in four stages using data from the stimulus material. This can include simple mathematical equations such as percentages and formulas you have learnt.

Understanding: this is for giving the formula for total revenue (AO1). This is worth 1 mark.

Application: this is for using the correct figures and working out the total revenue as directed by the question (AO2). This is worth up to 3 marks.

4 marks will be awarded for simply giving the correct answer.

> **Student A**
>
> 80 a × 300 b = 2,400 c

e **1/4 marks awarded** a The student uses the correct retail price, which is taken from the stimulus material, worth 1 AO2 mark. b This figure is missing a zero and therefore incorrectly states the quantity and is worth no marks. c As the quantity has been incorrectly stated this has also created the wrong total revenue figure and is worth no AO2 marks.

> **Student B**
>
> Total revenue = Quantity demanded × price a
>
> 80 b × 3,000 c = 240,000 d

e 3/4 marks awarded a The student gives the correct formula, worth 1 AO1 mark. b The student uses the correct retail price, which is taken from the stimulus material, but fails to use the pound sign, £, so does not score a mark. c The student uses the correct quantity demanded for 1 AO2 mark. d The student works out the accurate total revenue but again misses off the pound sign. However, as this has already lost a mark this would not be penalised so gains 1 AO2 mark.

Student A gains only 1 mark (a U grade) by forgetting to show the examiner the correct formula and by not accurately writing down the quantity. Student B gains 3 marks and gets a grade B. The fact that they put the figures in a different order to their formula will not lose any marks, though the lack of precision in terms of using the pound sign is careless and does lose an easy mark.

Demand

AS question only

Other than price, assess two factors that might cause a decrease in the demand for Magmatic's suitcases. (8 marks)

e The 'assess' command word means students need to supply an extract-based answer with advantages and disadvantages of the business concept. As the question is asking for two issues to be assessed, the highest skill practised is evaluation.

The mark allocations for this question are clear cut – they can be shown in this table:

	1st factor	2nd factor
Knowledge	1 mark	1 mark
Application	1 mark	1 mark
Analysis	1 mark	1 mark
Evaluation	1 mark	1 mark

The easiest way to persuade an examiner of your right to earn 8 marks is to write four short sentences for each factor. Each sentence should consciously try to hit one assessment objective at a time.

Level 1: this is for giving a reason why demand might decrease or a definition of demand. The student will not have used application correctly. There will be no advantages/disadvantages or they will be poorly discussed. This is worth a maximum of 2 marks, for example by giving two reasons.

Level 2: this is for giving a reason why demand might decrease or a definition of demand. The student will not have used application correctly. There will be an advantage or a disadvantage. This is worth up to 3 marks.

Level 3: this is for giving a reason why demand might decrease or a definition of demand. The student will not have used application correctly. There will be an advantage and a disadvantage, which have used application correctly. This is worth up to 3 marks.

Student A

One reason demand may decrease is that the price of the suitcases might go up so fewer customers can afford them. a

Another reason is consumer incomes have decreased, meaning that demand for the suitcases also reduces. b

e **2/8 marks awarded** a The student has recalled a factor, price, that can cause a decrease in demand to gain 1 mark and Level 1. b The student gives another factor that can affect demand, so gains 1 mark and Level 1 (2 so far). As the student hasn't explained why suitcase demand would decrease, there is no further mark awarded for either application or analysis. As the word 'suitcase' is in the stem of the question, this cannot be credited as context.

Student B

One factor that may cause a decrease in demand is a reduction in consumer incomes. a Extract A states that the Trunki suitcase is bought by middle-class families who have more income to purchase trendy bags for their children. b As a consequence of middle-class incomes reducing they have less money to spend on luxury Trunki suitcases so demand reduces. c This will result in not only less revenue from the number of cases sold but an increase in losses for Magmatic from the £1.4m. d

A second factor that can cause a decrease in demand is a drop in the use of complementary goods. [e] For the Trunki suitcase a complementary good would be holidays, so a fall in the demand for holidays would also mean a fall in the demand for suitcases as people only buy suitcases to go on holiday with. [f] A fall in demand for Trunkis would result in a lower number of cases sold and make Magmatic look at reducing its prices to compensate for this fall in demand. [g]

(e) **6/8 marks awarded** [a] The student has named a reason demand can decrease to gain 1 mark and Level 1. [b] The student has used context from the stimulus material to relate back to the reason, gaining 2 marks and Level 2 (3 so far). [c] The reason is explained as to an effect of demand, including further context from the stimulus material, and gains 1 mark and Level 2 (4 so far). [d] The student develops this effect, making the judgement that it would increase the company's losses, but as there is no balance, evaluation achieves 1 mark and Level 2 (5 so far).

[e] The student gives a second reason for demand decreasing but, as it is not yet developed, gains no further mark as all knowledge marks have been given. [f] The student relates the context in the stimulus material to the factor and also gives a consequence of the decrease in demand, gaining 1 mark and Level 3 (6 so far). [g] The student develops this consequence with context from the stimulus material, showing an element of judgement. However, as the student has not developed the consequence of the company reducing its prices, there is a lack of a balanced assessment in the answer, so no further marks can be awarded.

Student A did not develop the reasons given and made poor use of the stimulus material, meaning an E-grade answer at best. Student B gives an excellent answer, developing the causes and consequences of a decrease in demand using the stimulus material.

The most important point to note about questions that ask for 2 points is that you should think of the question as being in two parts, with equal marks for each part. Try not to use the same context from the stimulus material for each part as this may risk you not gaining the credit for the duplicated context. However, as the question states 'assess', the examiner is looking for a brief evaluation of both points. For example, the second factor considered by Student B could have been developed to show how a reduction in prices might help Trunki to maintain demand, but as the student failed to develop this type of argument they are limited to Level 3 and 6 marks, and a B. Points should be short and succinct but both factors need a brief evaluative point to score full marks.

On-the-job training

AS/A-level question

Magmatic is hiring new staff for its factory to make its new suitcase. Assess the likely impact on Magmatic of on-the-job training in helping to reduce costs. (10 marks)

ⓔ The 'assess' command word means students need to supply an extract-based answer with advantages and disadvantages of the business concept. The question is asking for problems for a business with on-the-job training, with the highest skill evidenced being evaluation. The relevant extract provided by the examiner should be referred to when answering the question.

Level 1: this is for giving a likely impact of on-the-job training or for a definition of the term. The student will not have used application correctly. There will be no advantages/disadvantages or they will be poorly discussed. This is worth a maximum of 2 marks, for example by giving a detailed definition of on-the-job training.

Level 2: this is for giving an implication of on-the-job training for the business. The student will have used application correctly. There will be an advantage or a disadvantage. This is worth up to 2 marks.

Level 3: this is for giving a reason why on-the-job training may be a benefit or a drawback for the business. The student will have used application correctly. There will be an advantage and a disadvantage, which have used application correctly. This is worth up to 2 marks.

Level 4: this is for giving a reason why on-the-job training may be a benefit or a drawback for the business. The student will have used application correctly. There will be an advantage and a disadvantage, which have been applied correctly. The advantages and disadvantages will link together and the evaluation will be detailed. A judgement or recommendation is made and explained. This is worth up to 4 marks.

> **Student A**
>
> On-the-job training is where the new staff would be shown how to make the products by other trained staff. **ⓐ** An advantage of on-the-job training is that it is cheaper than off-the-job training. **ⓑ** The business will not need to send the new member of staff to a separate training course, which would cost money, staff can train them in the new factory. **ⓒ**
>
> Another benefit is that the staff will learn how Magmatic wants its new suitcase made, including any unique ways current staff help speed up the process. **ⓓ** This will again save time and money and reduce staff costs. **ⓔ**
>
> Magmatic should therefore use on-the-job training as it reduces staff costs. **ⓕ**

ⓔ **5/10 marks awarded** **ⓐ** The student has stated a precise definition of on-the-job training to gain 1 mark and Level 1. **ⓑ** The student gives an advantage of on-the-job training but this is not developed and an assertion, so gains 1 mark and Level 1 (2 marks so far). **ⓒ** The advantage is not developed and has very weak analysis with weak context, so gains 2 marks and Level 2 (4 so far). **ⓓ** The student states an advantage which has sufficient context and analysis to gain 1 mark and Level 3 (5 so far). **ⓔ** This point lacks any developed analysis and context and gains no marks. **ⓕ** The student attempts a judgement which lacks any further development and gains no marks.

Student B

One likely impact of using on-the-job training is that they will benefit from demonstration of the task as they work from staff with skills to create the Jurni suitcase, who are already efficient at making the product. a As a consequence, staff will not need to go away from the factory to learn the skills in a classroom environment, thus saving Magmatic travel time and expenses for staff to attend this venue. b Coaching will also help reduce staff costs as new staff members will learn how to make the suitcase, such as the skateboard wheels, while on the job with other staff members encouraging to become more productive. c This means that Magmatic will save money on each Jurni made as even new staff will be able to produce parts of the suitcase in faster times. d

However, on-the-job training means the staff who take time out to train new staff are not as productive in making the Jurni as they now have to multi task, sharing their time between training and actual making of the product. e This means that any potential savings from training at the factory would be lost as the product is not being made as quickly by current employees, actually increasing the costs. f

To reduce the risks of on-the-job training, staff undertaking the training should be given the extra time on the production line to ensure new staff get the right level of coaching and instruction. g Staff doing training also need to be checked to make sure they have the right skills and do not pass on poor methods of producing the suitcase. h This will ensure the benefits of on-the-job training are maximised, resulting in Magmatic minimising staff costs and maximising profits to ensure the Jurni turns current losses of £1.4m into a profit in the longer term. i

e **10/10 marks awarded** a The student has stated a possible impact on the business, also relating this to the context of the stimulus material. The student also starts to analyse the benefit for the business but this is not developed, meaning 3 marks and Level 2. b The student then develops the benefit, giving a correct consequence with context, gaining 2 marks and Level 3 (5 so far). c A further impact of coaching is given, together with context and developed analysis, gaining 1 mark and Level 3 (6 so far). d The student develops their analysis but as they have already achieved maximum marks for Level 3, this gains no further marks. e The student gives a disadvantage of on-the-job training with context, but as it lacks development gains 1 mark and Level 4 (7 so far). f The student develops the evaluative point in detail, gaining 1 mark and Level 4 (8 so far). g The student makes a recommendation about on-the-job training to counter its problems, but as this is not developed sufficiently it gains no further mark. h The student develops their recommendation to give a judgement worth 1 mark and Level 4 (9 so far). i The student gives a contextual conclusion and judgement taking into account their recommendation for 1 mark and Level 4 (10 in total).

Student A gives a weak analysis with context of on-the-job training, gaining a C grade. The student makes a common mistake of giving only a one-sided argument with no judgement or conclusion. Student B gives an excellent contextual evaluation of on-the-job training. The student uses the context very well by developing the stimulus material to give reasoned examples of the problems that could arise for on-the-job training, gaining an A.

Distribution channels

AS question

Magmatic is considering changing how it can achieve greater profit maximisation by distributing its products through retail stores or through the use of internet stores.

Evaluate these two options and recommend which is the more suitable for a business such as Magmatic.
(20 marks)

🄴 The 'evaluate' command word means you need to review the pros and cons of the business term using stimulus material. Weigh up strengths and weaknesses of arguments and then support a specific judgement, forming a recommendation and conclusion. Extracts B and C can be used to provide application, but the words 'such as' in the question mean the student can base their application on any similar business.

Level 1: this is for giving a reason why the business would choose the internet or a retail store as a distribution channel or a definition or some knowledge of distribution. The student will not have used application correctly. There will be no advantages/disadvantages or they will be poorly discussed. This is worth a maximum of 4 marks, for example by giving detailed definitions of distribution.

Level 2: this is for giving a reason why the business would choose the internet or a retail store as a distribution channel or a definition or some knowledge of distribution. The student will have used application correctly. There will be an advantage or a disadvantage of the different distribution channels but they will be poorly developed. This is worth up to 4 marks.

Level 3: this is for giving a reason why the business would choose the internet or a retail store as a distribution channel or a definition or some knowledge of distribution. The student will have used application correctly. There will be an advantage and a disadvantage, which have used application correctly for the use of internet stores or the use of retail stores. There may be evaluation of the internet or retail stores as a suitable distribution channel to create greater profit maximisation, but it is poorly developed. This is worth up to 6 marks.

Level 4: this is for giving a reason why the business would choose the internet or a retail store as a distribution channel or a definition or some knowledge of distribution. The student will have used application correctly. There will be an advantage and a disadvantage which have been applied correctly for the use of internet stores or the use of retail stores. The advantages and disadvantages of the retail store and/or the internet store as a distribution channel will link together coherently and the evaluation will be detailed and wide ranging. A judgement and recommendation will be made about the best approach for the business to achieve the objective of maximising profit, with a conclusion. This is worth up to 6 marks.

Student A

Distribution channels are ways in which to get finished products to customers. **a** This includes producer to wholesaler and then to retailer. **b** A producer is a business that makes, grows or supplies goods or commodities for sale. A wholesaler is a business that acts as a link between the producer and retailer that buys in bulk and sells to resellers rather than to customers. **c** A retailer is a business that sells goods or services directly to the customer. **d**

Magmatic's using a range of distribution channels means they can sell some of their products through a wholesaler, some through a retailer and some straight to the customer. Selling straight to the customer is called direct marketing. **e**

The benefit to Magmatic of selling through a retailer is the retailer can sell small quantities of the suitcases to customers in the area where they live. **f** This benefits the customer as they don't have to travel far to buy the product and will have a range of suitcases to choose from. **g**

The benefit of Magmatic selling through a wholesaler is they can sell larger numbers to the wholesaler who can then distribute these to local shops. Magmatic benefit as they can make a larger amount of money by selling to the wholesaler in bulk. **h**

Magmatic can sell direct to the customer as they already do for the current suitcase. **i** This benefits the customer because they don't have to visit a physical retail store, saving them time and money. **j** However, there are many other online shops that sell suitcases so customers will be able to choose the cheapest product. **k**

Magmatic should sell online as it is cheaper and quicker for the customer to buy a suitcase. **l**

e **7/20 marks awarded** **a** The student gives a definition of distribution channels for 1 mark and Level 1. **b–d** The definition is expanded on three times, being worth 3 marks and Level 1 (4 so far). **e** The student develops the definition further and gives some very weak context, so as the maximum of 4 Level 1 marks have already been awarded, no further marks can be given. **f** The student gives a benefit of one distribution channel with some context, but as this is not yet developed into a context for Magmatic gains 1 mark and Level 2 (5 so far). **g** The student now gives benefits to the customer rather than for the business and as this is not answering the question gains no further mark or level. **h** The student gives another benefit but this has no context and is an assumption so gains 2 marks and Level 2 (7 so far). **i** A benefit is given of selling to customers but this gains no credit as it is not yet developed. **j** A further benefit is attempted but not explained sufficiently to gain a further mark. **k** The student again gives the benefit for the customer but not for Magmatic so gains no further mark. **l** The student attempts to make a conclusion but as this is very general and based on the benefits for the customer, not Magmatic, it gains no further marks.

Student B

Distribution channels are ways in which to get finished products to customers. a The extract tells us that Magmatic have already established a number of distribution channels including an online shop to sell their Trunki cases and through stores such as M&S. b

One benefit of having different distribution channels is that it meets the needs of different types of customers. c For example, selling to 'middle-class parents' may mean this segment of the market prefer a more trendy type of selling experience, so Magmatic as the producer of the Trunki could sell to M&S, the retailer, as this store is seen as being very reliable and fashionable for this type of customer. d There is a large network of stores already set up, meaning that customers are likely to have access to the suitcases at a shop near to where they live. e As a consequence, Magmatic can sell a large amount of suitcases to M&S and benefit both from their brand enhancing their own brand's reputation and do not have the large extra costs of having to set up their own shops around the UK. f

However, the disadvantage of this approach is that M&S are likely to want to buy the suitcases at a discount as they are buying in bulk. g This means that Magmatic will make less profit on each suitcase, for example instead of selling the Jurni at £80 they might have to sell it to M&S at £70. h

A benefit of Magmatic also selling Trunki and Jurni suitcases through an online store would be to allow customers who are not near one of the M&S stores to still buy the suitcase. i Not only does this mean Magmatic will have access to a much wider range of customers but they can keep all the profit they make rather than the retailer having to take a cut of it. j However, there are many online retailers selling suitcases and one of the reasons Magmatic is making a loss of £1.4m is it has lots of businesses copying the suitcases and selling them. k Using an online store may risk this problem getting worse and if customers believe they are getting a similar product but for a cheaper price they might actually buy online from another shop, reducing sales and potentially damaging their brand image, due to the fakes' poor quality, and ultimately reducing profits. l

The online store has been successful and an expansion of this distribution channel can help Magmatic expand quicker than through physical retailers to meet their profit maximisation objective. m

(e) **18/20 marks awarded** [a] The student has given a relevant definition which is worth 1 mark and Level 1. [b] The student relates distribution channels to the stimulus material, developing the answer and gaining 4 marks and Level 2 (5 so far). [c] The student names a benefit of different distribution channels but this is not yet developed enough to gain further marks. [d] The student develops a benefit of using a specific distribution channel using context, though it is weak development so gains 3 marks and Level 2 (8 marks so far). [e] This benefit is further developed in terms of the benefit to the customer and not Magmatic, so no further marks are awarded. [f] The student develops a positive consequence for Magmatic of a distribution channel in context, implying profits will increase, and gains 2 marks and Level 3 (10 marks so far). [g] The student gives a disadvantage of the distribution channel in context but it is not developed and gains 3 marks and Level 3 (13 marks so far). [h] The student develops this into an evaluative point with good context and gains 1 mark and Level 3 (14 marks so far). [i,j] The student develops a benefit of another distribution channel with context and related to profit, gaining 2 marks and Level 4 (16 marks so far). [k,l] The student gives a risk of using online distribution with strong context and refers to MOPS in terms of the market and the brand, gaining 2 marks and Level 4 (18 marks). [m] The student attempts to make a judgement but it is not particularly strong so doesn't gain a further mark.

Student A spends too much time discussing definitions, which are worth few marks. The student also misinterprets the question and answers it in terms of benefits for the customer rather than solely for Magmatic and its profit maximisation objective. This is rectified later in the answer but they make the same mistake for their evaluative point. The judgement and conclusion are too weak to be awarded any marks, with the student scoring an E grade. The key to writing a good answer to the 20-mark question is to evaluate both options in relation to the focus of the question, in this case profit maximisation for Magmatic.

Student B spends little time in gaining marks for analysis and evaluative points. The answer could be a little more concise, which would have given them more time to develop a strong judgement and conclusion. As the question asks for a range of channels, the minimum to score full marks is to discuss two, which this student does. The skill is to do this as succinctly as possible. The student also should have focused explicitly on profit maximisation at the start of the answer. The command words must appear frequently in your answer to ensure the examiner gives you credit. This student gains an A grade.

3 Umbro sportswear

Extract A

Umbro is a globally recognised football brand with a strong heritage derived from more than 70 years' association with the sport of football. Umbro designs, sources and markets football-related apparel, footwear and equipment and its products are sold in over 90 countries worldwide. Based in the UK, the Umbro business was founded in 1924. All products are sourced from independent manufacturers, principally located in the Far East. The brand has lost out in market share in the last few years to Nike and Adidas in lucrative sponsorship deals and has had moved into third place as a global brand for football clothing. Umbro has few managers and prefers staff to work independently and creatively to help keep ahead of competitors.

Umbro currently supplies playing and training kit to the Republic of Ireland national football team. Umbro and its relevant international licensees supply kit to leading professional clubs worldwide, including PS Eindhoven (the Netherlands), West Ham and Everton (England). The Umbro brand is also endorsed by high-profile individual players including Real Madrid defender Pepe along with Tottenham's Eric Dier.

Source: BBC news, www.bbc.co.uk/news/business-20075681

Extract B

The supply schedule for Umbro trainers manufactured in Taiwan

Price per pair (£)	Quantity supplied
5	20
10	40
15	60
20	80
25	100

In order to try to cut costs Umbro has outsourced its manufacturing of trainers from Taiwan to China. The forecasted saving in production is 10%.

Extract C

Internationally, the Group operates principally through a network of 47 licensees who source and distribute products to sports retail customers. The Group works closely with its international licensees to maintain a global and uniform Umbro brand identity.

The global markets for sports apparel and footwear increasingly overlap with the leisurewear market and Umbro is positioning its range of product lines to benefit from this convergence. Umbro was recently sold by owner Nike to Iconix Brand Group, which has sports and designer clothing brands.

UK population in thousands

Age	1981	1991	1997	2035
19 or under	16,337	14,800	14,970	16,892
20–64	31,544	33,907	34,770	36,352
65 plus	8,472	9,099	9,269	19,956
Total	**56,353**	**57,806**	**59,009**	**73,200**

Span of control and collective bargaining

AS question

What is meant by a narrow span of control? (2 marks)

e The 'what is meant by' command words mean you need a definition of the business term in the question and either this can be developed or an example can be given.

Understanding: of what is meant by narrow span of control (AO1). This is worth up to 2 marks and can include an enhanced definition or a basic definition and an example of narrow span of control as long as it relates back to the definition.

Accurate definitions are critical for marks.

> **Student A**
>
> A narrow span of control is the opposite to Umbro as they have a wide span of control because in the extract it says there are few managers. **a**

e **0/2 marks awarded** **a** The student has attempted to relate a relevant part of the stimulus material to the business term, but it does not clearly relate to what a narrow span of control means in this context so gains no marks.

> **Student B**
>
> A narrow span of control means that employees will have fewer decision-making powers in the business. **a**

e **1/2 marks awarded** **a** The student has given a definition of a narrow span of control for 1 AO1 mark.

For Student A to score 0 marks (grade U) shows they don't clearly understand the requirement of the question. The attempt to use the stimulus material could have gained a mark if it had contrasted narrow with wide span of control. Student B shows a lack of understanding of what the question requires for a second mark so gains a D grade.

What is meant by collective bargaining? (2 marks)

e The 'what is meant by' command words mean you need a definition of the business term in the question and either this can be developed or an example can be given from the stimulus material related back to the definition.

Understanding: of what is meant by collective bargaining (AO1). This is worth up to 2 marks and can include an enhanced definition or a basic definition and an example of collective bargaining as long as it relates back to the definition.

Accurate definitions are critical for marks.

> **Student A**
>
> Collective bargaining is where an individual negotiates their terms and conditions of employment with their employer. ⓐ As Umbro encourage employees to be creative they would negotiate their own pay rise if they had been successful at work. ⓑ

ⓔ **0/2 marks awarded** ⓐ The student confuses collective bargaining with individual negotiation and gains no marks. ⓑ The student reinforces this mistake by giving an example of individual negotiation and gains no marks.

> **Student B**
>
> Collective bargaining is where a business negotiates with representatives of employees, such as trade unions, regarding the terms and conditions of employment. ⓐ For Umbro the trade union representing the employees might negotiate for a wage rise which all those covered by the collective bargain can benefit from. ⓑ

ⓔ **2/2 marks awarded** ⓐ The student has given a precise definition of collective bargaining for 1 AO1 mark. ⓑ The student develops the definition and gives an example of the type of negotiation covered by collective bargaining, worth 1 AO1 mark.

Student A confuses the term in the question with individual bargaining and misses out on 2 easy marks (grade U). Student B scores 2 marks (grade A) by giving an accurate definition and development of this – but the answer is longer than it would ideally be. Time is tight in the AS exam in particular.

Supply

AS/A-level question

Using the data from Extract B, construct a supply diagram to illustrate the impact of Umbro's decision to move manufacturing of trainers to China. (4 marks)

ⓔ The 'using 'and 'construct' command words mean you must complete a diagram from data and information in the stimulus material.

Understanding: for correct construction of the supply curve and correctly labelling the axes, price and quantity (AO1). This is worth 2 marks.

Application: for correctly interpreting the shift in the supply curve to the right (AO2). This is worth 1 mark.

Analysis: for labelling and showing the increase in quantity supplied at the same price on the supply diagram (AO3). This is worth 1 mark.

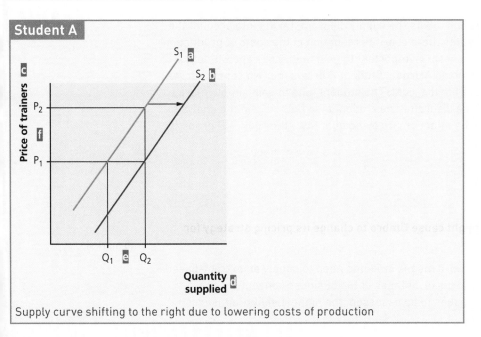

Supply curve shifting to the right due to lowering costs of production

e **4/4 marks awarded** **a,b** The student correctly constructs the two supply curves and gains 1 AO1 mark. The student correctly interprets the shift in the supply curve to the right and gains 1 AO2 mark. **c,d** The student correctly labels the axes Price and Quantity and gains 1 AO1 mark. **e,f** The student correctly draws the effect on price and quantity of a shift in the supply curve to the right and gains 1 AO3 mark.

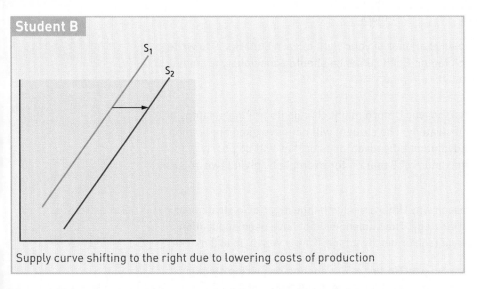

Supply curve shifting to the right due to lowering costs of production

e **2/4 marks awarded** **a,b** The student correctly constructs the two supply curves and gains 1 AO mark. **a** The student correctly interprets the shift in the supply curve to the right and gains 1 AO2 mark. As the student has added no further labels to the diagram, there are no additional marks awarded.

Student A correctly draws and labels the supply diagram, taking into account the stimulus material which states there is a 10% reduction in the costs of production in China. Labelling of the diagram is important to gain full marks and Student A completes this in full, gaining an A grade. Student B draws the two supply curves and correctly labels the shift to the right. The student fails to gain simple marks through omitting to label the diagram. The student also fails to gain the analysis mark by omitting to draw the effect on price and quantity – they gain a D grade for simple omissions.

Pricing strategy

AS question

Assess two factors that might cause Umbro to change its pricing strategy for trainers. (8 marks)

ⓔ The 'assess' command word means students need to supply an extract-based answer with advantages and disadvantages of the business concept. As the question is asking for two issues to be assessed, the highest skill practised is evaluation.

The mark allocations for this question are clear cut – they can be shown in this table:

	1st factor	2nd factor
Knowledge	1 mark	1 mark
Application	1 mark	1 mark
Analysis	1 mark	1 mark
Evaluation	1 mark	1 mark

The easiest way to persuade an examiner of your right to earn 8 marks is to write four short sentences for each factor. Each sentence should consciously try to hit one assessment objective at a time.

Level 1: this is for giving a reason why Umbro might change its pricing strategy or a definition of pricing/pricing strategy. The student will not have used application correctly. There will be no advantages/disadvantages or they will be poorly discussed. This is worth a maximum of 2 marks, for example by giving two reasons.

Level 2: this is for giving a reason why Umbro might change its pricing strategy or a definition of pricing/pricing strategy. The student will not have used application correctly. There will be an advantage or disadvantage. This is worth up to 3 marks.

Level 3: this is for giving a reason why Umbro might change its pricing strategy or a definition of pricing/pricing strategy. The student will have used application correctly. There will be an advantage and disadvantage which have used application correctly. This is worth up to 3 marks.

Student A

Price is the amount the business charges the customer for the product or service. [a] One factor that might cause Umbro to change their pricing strategy is that they may want to sell more products. [b] To do this they could change to a penetration pricing strategy. [c] This would make the products cheaper than its competitors and encourage customers to switch to the Umbro brand. [d]

Another factor might be that they want to make more profit across their range so they go for a price strategy that guarantees a profit margin on each product. [e] This would mean switching to cost plus pricing which has a mark-up added to the cost of producing the item. [f] The advantage to Umbro is they can justify price increases to the customer when their own costs of producing the product go up. [g]

(e) **5/8 marks awarded** [a] The student defines price when the question asks for pricing strategy or pricing, so gains no marks. [b] The student gives an appropriate factor and gains 1 mark and Level 1. [c] The student identifies a pricing strategy to gain a further 1 mark and Level 1 (2 so far). [d] The student analyses the effect of penetration pricing on Umbro but without any context or development so gains 1 mark and Level 2 (3 so far). [e,f] The student identifies another pricing strategy and gains 1 mark and Level 2 (4 so far). [g] The student gives an advantage of this pricing strategy but this does not link to the context of the business so gains 1 mark and Level 2 (5 in total).

Student B

One factor that might change Umbro's pricing strategy is the fall in the strength of its brand compared to Adidas and Nike. [a] As Umbro have got less sponsorship deals customers may feel the brand is not worth a premium price, where customers are willing to pay more for a football shirt, than competitors charge. [b] As a consequence, Umbro may have to adopt a more competitive price which is similar to others in the market, which will mean less profit per product sold and lower profits overall. [c]

(e) **4/8 marks awarded** [a] The student identifies a reason why Umbro may change its pricing strategy and gains 1 mark and Level 1. Even though there is context, the student does not use this to develop their answer so gains no further marks. [b] The student then analyses the change in price using the context of the stimulus material but this is not developed enough to form a consequence and so gains 2 marks and Level 2 (3 so far). [c] The student gives a consequence of the new pricing strategy for profits and gains 1 mark and Level 2 (4 in total).

Student A makes the error of not using any context from the stimulus material to relate pricing strategy to the answer, missing out on marks. They also fail to develop the advantages, missing out on 1 mark and therefore gaining a C grade, when the score could easily have been much higher. Student B fails to understand that the question requires two factors and thus attempts only one. They needed to develop their point further and therefore gained only a D grade, even though the use of context is better than Student A's.

Motivational theory

AS and A-level question

Assess the likely impact on Umbro's staff if managers adopt Herzberg's theory of motivation to work towards profit maximisation.

(10 marks)

ⓔ The 'assess' command word means students need to supply an extract-based answer with advantages and disadvantages of the business concept. The question is asking for problems for a business with motivational theory, with the highest skill evidenced being evaluation. The relevant extract provided by the examiner should be referred to when answering the question.

Level 1: this is for giving a likely impact of Herzberg's theory of motivation or a definition of the theory. The student will not have used application correctly. There will be no advantages/disadvantages or they will be poorly discussed. This is worth a maximum of 2 marks, for example by giving a detailed definition of Herzberg's theory of motivation.

Level 2: this is for giving a likely impact of Herzberg's theory of motivation or a definition of the theory. The student will have used application correctly. There will be an advantage or a disadvantage. This is worth up to 2 marks.

Level 3: this is for giving a likely impact of Herzberg's theory of motivation or a definition of the theory. The student will have used application correctly. There will be an advantage and disadvantage which have used application correctly. This is worth up to 2 marks.

Level 4: this is for giving a likely impact of Herzberg's theory of motivation or a definition of the theory. The student will have used application correctly. There will be an advantage and disadvantage which have used application correctly. The advantages and disadvantages will link together and the evaluation will be detailed. A judgement or recommendation is made and explained. This is worth up to 4 marks.

Student A

Herzberg's theory says there are certain factors that a business can introduce that would directly motivate employees to work harder. ⓐ These are called motivators and include ensuring employees are satisfied with their job. ⓑ Herzberg also said to ensure employees are motivated the employer has to ensure hygiene factors do not get in the way of this. ⓒ For example, if the employees aren't paid properly this would be a hygiene factor and demotivate staff. ⓓ

An advantage of using Herzberg's theory of motivation is that employees will become more productive as areas that could cause conflicts with the employer are satisfied, for example the employees get a pay rise they want. ⓔ This would help Umbro as if employees are more motivated they will make more products. This means Umbro will make more profit. ⓕ

A disadvantage of Herzberg's theory is that employees will soon get used to their new pay and then want more, creating either more conflict or increasing the costs to the employer. ⓖ Increased costs will reduce profits. ⓗ

e **5/10 marks awarded** a The student gives a basic definition of Herzberg's theory for 1 mark and Level 1. b The definition is developed for 1 mark and Level 1 (2 so far). c,d The student develops the definition in more detail but gains no further marks as there are only 2 Level 1 marks available. e The student gives an advantage of Herzberg's theory without context so gains 1 mark and Level 2 (3 so far). f The advantage is developed but as it lacks any context that is unique to the stimulus material and is weak, it gains only 1 mark and Level 2 (4 so far). g The student attempts to evaluate Herzberg's theory but it contains assumptions which are not explained in detail, meaning it gains 1 more mark and Level 3 (5 so far). h The student makes a broad assumption lacking any explanation and gains no further mark.

Student B

Herzberg's theory of motivation has two factors. a Motivators are those factors that an employer like Umbro can promote to help employees feel valued such as the chances of promotion. b According to Extract A, Umbro wants staff to be creative so they might offer staff a promotion if they come up with new ways of gaining sponsorship deals with individual players such as Eric Dier. c As a consequence Umbro will improve their brand image and this will encourage customers to buy more shirts, increasing profits. d

Herzberg also states that hygiene factors need to be met to ensure employees don't become dissatisfied. e For example, staff need to be given what they believe is reasonable pay. f Staff in the new factory could be offered piece rate so that the more trainers they produce, the more they get paid, meaning there could be greater savings in the costs of production as well as staff being satisfied with the amount they get paid. g This means Umbro will have well-motivated staff and as costs of production are likely to reduce they will make more profit on the sale of trainers. h

---

e **6/10 marks awarded** a The student gives a basic definition of Herzberg's theory for 1 mark and Level 1. b The definition is developed for 1 mark and Level 1 (2 so far). c The student uses the stimulus material to relate to motivators, gaining 1 mark and Level 2 (3 so far). d The student gives a benefit of using Herzberg's theory in context and relates it to Umbro's profits, gaining 3 marks and Level 3 (6 so far). e,f The student gives further knowledge points on Herzberg's theory but gains no further mark as the maximum marks for Level 1 have been reached. g The student uses context from the stimulus material correctly, but as this adds no development to the answer, no further marks are awarded. h The student gives a benefit of Herzberg's theory on hygiene factors in context, but as there has been no evaluation before, this gains no further marks.

Student A makes a typical error of spending a lot of time defining relevant concepts when there is only a maximum of 2 marks available. They also fail to use the stimulus material, which would have helped gain higher marks, together with better development of their points. Even though there is an evaluative point, the answer is weak and gains a D grade. Student B uses the stimulus material well to back up their analytical points but fails to do any evaluation, achieving a C grade. To gain high marks, evaluation, for example a disadvantage of Herzberg's theory related to Umbro, must be included.

Intrapreneurship

A-level question

Assess the likely impact on Umbro's success of encouraging greater intrapreneurship among its employees. (12 marks)

ⓔ The 'assess' command word means students need to supply an extract-based answer with advantages and disadvantages of the business concept. They also need to make a judgement about the business term in the context of the extract and include other relevant business theories. The relevant extract can be used to provide application but the words 'such as' in the question mean the student can base their application on any similar business.

Level 1: this is for giving a likely impact of intrapreneurship on Umbro or a definition of intrapreneurship. The student will not have used application correctly. There will be no advantages/disadvantages or they will be poorly discussed. This is worth a maximum of 2 marks, for example defining intrapreneurship.

Level 2: this is for giving a likely impact of intrapreneurship on Umbro or a definition of intrapreneurship. The student will have used application correctly. There will be an advantage or disadvantage. This is worth up to 2 marks.

Level 3: this is for giving a likely impact of intrapreneurship on Umbro or a definition of intrapreneurship. The student will have used application correctly. There will be an advantage and a disadvantage which have used application correctly. This is worth up to 4 marks.

Level 4: this is for giving a likely impact of intrapreneurship on Umbro or a definition of intrapreneurship. The student will have used application correctly. There will be an advantage and a disadvantage which have used application correctly. The advantages and disadvantages will link together and the evaluation will be coherent and wide ranging. A judgement will be made about the business term in the context of the question. This is worth up to 4 marks.

Student A

An intrapreneur is someone within a business who takes risks in an effort to solve a given problem. ⓐ This means that managers and staff are allowed to take risks in order to help Umbro become more successful. ⓑ The extract states Umbro have few managers and encourage staff to be creative. ⓒ Umbro could improve their brand image by allowing staff to look at innovative ways to advertise their products such as using viral marketing. ⓓ Viral marketing is a way of advertising on social media using catchy adverts that Umbro customers would see as trendy. ⓔ Intrapreneurship would allow staff to use this type of marketing in a way that suits their customers as Umbro has customers in over 90 countries. ⓕ Staff in these countries could use different viral marketing campaigns to meet the needs of customers in individual countries and this unique selling point would give Umbro a competitive advantage in terms of brand awareness and their competitors such as Nike. ⓖ As a consequence

---

intrapreneurship would allow Umbro to become much more market orientated in each country they operate in, improving their brand awareness with customers, tempting them to buy more sportswear and Umbro capturing more market share. h

However, a risk with intrapreneurship is that Umbro give too much power to local staff to make decisions and this means that decisions in one country about the marketing of the product may be in conflict with what is being done in another country. i For example, PSV Eindhoven and Umbro's sponsorship of the club could be for a lot more money than West Ham in the UK. j As a consequence, gaining sponsorship deals will become more and more difficult as they will cost more money as clubs learn there are better deals to be had. k Umbro would gain more clubs but at too big a cost. l

Umbro should encourage intrapreneurship as it will help the company to benefit from the local knowledge of employees when marketing the product. m But the risks need to be controlled by giving employees clear boundaries as to what creative ideas they can put into practice and which ideas need to be discussed by senior managers of Umbro. n This would create a balanced trade-off between using the creativity of the workforce to improve profits through intrapreneurship but not at the loss of longer-term profit. o

e **12/12 marks awarded** a The student gives a definition of intrapreneurship, gaining 1 mark and Level 1. b The student develops the definition to gain 1 mark and Level 1 (2 marks so far). c The student relates the context to intrapreneurship, gaining 1 mark and Level 2 (3 so far). d The student gives a weak benefit of intrapreneurship, gaining no mark. e The student uses a marketing concept to develop the benefit of intrapreneurship but has not fully developed it, so no marks. f A benefit of intrapreneurship is fully developed in context, giving 3 marks and Level 3 (6 so far). g,h The benefit to Umbro is further developed in context using MOPS, gaining 1 mark and Level 3 (7 so far). i The student gives a risk of intrapreneurship with context but weak development so gains only 1 mark and Level 3 (8 so far). j–l The student develops the risk of allowing intrapreneurship to aid Umbro's success in detail and in context, gaining 2 marks and Level 4 (10 so far). m The student makes a recommendation about Umbro using intrapreneurship, gaining 1 mark and Level 4 (11 so far). n,o The student gives a judgement using MOPS, gaining 1 mark and Level 4 (12 in total).

Student B

Intrapreneurship is allowing employees to be creative in a business and solve problems. a This can include thinking of ways to improve profits or meeting customer needs locally. b Umbro can benefit from intrapreneurship by allowing local staff in the 90 countries more freedom to respond to customer needs and wants. c For example, if customers want lower-priced football kit for West Ham the member of staff would be able to come up with a creative way to meet this need. d

The problem with intrapreneurship is that employees may take their good ideas and go into business themselves, with the business losing control of the profits they could have made from this idea. e For example, if the member of staff finds a cheaper supplier of kit they would decide to go into business by themselves and sell it to the club and customers. ⓘ This means Umbro would lose profits from the customers. ⓖ

Umbro should not allow intrapreneurship as it is too dangerous for their profits. ⓗ

ⓔ **5/12 marks awarded** ⓐ The student gives a definition of intrapreneurship, gaining 1 mark and Level 1. ⓑ The student develops this definition to gain 1 mark and Level 1 (2 so far). ⓒⓓ The student uses context to give a benefit of Umbro allowing intrapreneurship, but it is not developed well so gains 2 marks and Level 2 (4 so far). ⓔ The student gives a theoretical disadvantage of intrapreneurship and gains 1 mark and Level 3 (5 so far). ⓕⓖ The student appears to develop their disadvantage in context. However, as what the student suggests shows poor understanding of branding, no marks are awarded. ⓗ The student simply makes an assumption, which gains no marks.

Student A gains full marks and an A grade by making excellent use of the stimulus material and a wide range of business theory together with a recommendation and a balanced judgement. Student B fails to develop the benefit of intrapreneurship in the context of the question. They discuss a potential problem with the concept but do not show a practical understanding of branding by saying that staff 'would' take a course of action, gaining no high marks for analysis. If they had used 'could' this might have gained extra marks, but the student's answer gets only a D grade.

Demographic trends

AS question

Umbro is considering developing its market share in the 16–25 or the 50+ age group demographic.

Evaluate these two options and recommend which may be the more profitable for a business such as Umbro.

(20 marks)

ⓔ The 'evaluate' command word means you need to review the pros and cons of the business term using stimulus material. Weigh up strengths and weaknesses of arguments and then support a specific judgement, forming a recommendation and conclusion. Extract C can be used to provide application but the words 'such as' in the question mean the student can base their application on any similar business.

Level 1: this is for giving a reason, a definition or some knowledge of the demographic trends or defining demographic trends. The student will not have used application correctly. There will be no advantages/disadvantages or they will be poorly discussed. This is worth a maximum of 4 marks, for example by giving detailed definitions of demographic trends or market research.

Level 2: this is for giving a reason, a definition or some knowledge of the demographic trends or defining demographic trends. The student will have used application correctly. There will be an advantage or disadvantage of the demographic trends but it will be poorly developed. This is worth up to 4 marks.

Level 3: this is for giving a reason, a definition or some knowledge of the demographic trends or defining demographic trends. The student will have used application correctly. There will be an advantage and a disadvantage for demographic trends which has been applied to profitability correctly. There may be evaluation of the demographic trends and profitability but it is poorly developed. This is worth up to 6 marks.

Level 4: this is for giving a reason, a definition or some knowledge of the demographic trends or defining demographic trends. The student will have used application correctly. There will be an advantage and a disadvantage for demographic trends which has been applied to profitability correctly. The advantages and disadvantages of the demographic trends will link together, coherently, to evaluate each option's profitability for Umbro, and the evaluation will be detailed and wide ranging. A judgement and recommendation will be made about the best approach for the business to achieve the objective of profitability, with a conclusion. This is worth up to 6 marks.

Using Extract C data from the stimulus material is particularly important for gaining a high mark in this question as it shows demographic trends.

Student A

Demographic trends are statistics about human beings such as age and marital status. a One advantage of using demographic trends is that they help a business make decisions about potential or actual changes taking place in terms of their customers and the products they sell to them. b In the extract the population in the UK is increasing and there is forecast to be more people aged 65 and over. c As people are becoming more active this means that Umbro may be able to make sports clothing that meets the needs of this type of customer. d As a consequence this may give Umbro a competitive advantage over other businesses such as Nike and it may gain market share and more profits from this segment of the market. e

However, the problem with demographic trends is that the information is available to all businesses as it is secondary market research. f The implication to Umbro is that Nike and Adidas will also know that those aged 50 and above will be increasing in number up to 2035. g This means that as all businesses in this market have the same access to the data it will depend on how quickly Umbro acts compared to Adidas as to whether they have any competitive advantage in launching sports equipment aimed at the new age group. h As Nike and Adidas are the market leaders and Umbro appears to have lost some of its competitive edge, it is more likely they will gain the competitive advantage with making sportswear for this age group, risking losing market share and ultimately profits. i

In conclusion, Umbro will need to make sure they use the demographic trends data before Adidas and Nike if they are to gain any advantage in meeting the needs of the new market segment of older customers and in the longer term market share and profits. j

ⓔ 12/20 marks awarded ⓐ The student gives a definition of demographic trends, gaining 1 mark and Level 1. ⓑ A benefit of using demographic trends is explained but has no context, so gains 2 marks and Level 2 (3 marks so far). ⓒ–ⓔ The benefit is developed using context and other business terms to answer the question in terms of both demographic trends and profits, gaining 4 marks and Level 2 (7 so far). ⓕ A problem with demographic trends is given but has no context or development, resulting in 1 mark and Level 2 (8 so far). ⓖ–ⓘ The student develops the problem with demographic trends with context and relating it to the issue of profitability, gaining 3 marks and Level 3 (11 marks). ⓙ The student attempts to provide a conclusion and recommendation, but as this is weak and undeveloped it gains 1 mark and Level 3 (12 marks).

Student B

Demographic trends indicate the changes in population size and structure over time. ⓐ In this case, the trend indicated in the table clearly shows how the UK population is ageing, with a declining number of individuals in the 19 years and under section. ⓑ These fall from 16,377,000 to 14,970,000 between 1981 and 1997. ⓒ Although, balancing the reduction in younger people, is the growth in the 20–64-year-old and 65-plus sector. ⓓ This latter group is growing significantly, from 8,472,000 to 9,269,000 by 1997. These trends are set to continue to 2021. ⓔ The implications of these trends on Umbro, who manufactures primarily sportswear, such as replica football kits, are they appear to face a shrinking market over time. ⓕ This is because younger consumers are likely to be their main market segment. ⓖ It is this age group which tends to be more active in sports and thus represents a greater market for such goods. ⓗ

As a consequence, Umbro face possibly a steady decline in sales of their sportswear in line with the falling population of younger, under-19 consumers, which ultimately leads to lower profitability. ⓘ Umbro may decide to broaden their portfolio of sportswear to tempt older consumers – an age group which is clearly expanding. ⓙ This may help compensate for a decline in their main target market. ⓚ Umbro may introduce an entirely redesigned range aimed at the more mature end of the market, targeting much older individuals. ⓛ Thus enabling Umbro to appeal to a wider age range of consumers, helping to preserve or even increases its sales levels and profit levels in the UK. ⓜ

However, it would be wrong to assume that Umbro would suffer from a shrinking market based on the figures above. ⓝ Demographic trends are figures only for population and give no hint to the levels of popularity of football. ⓞ Even if the trends were to be accurate then there is no accounting for the percentage of potential football fans within this age group. ⓟ With the introduction of all-seater stadiums, Sky Television and the growing popularity of women's football, it seems that the popularity of the sport is increasing year on year. ⓠ The extract also makes it clear that Umbro operate in 90 countries, not just the UK. ⓡ Therefore if the number of football fans both abroad and within the 20 years and under UK figures increased by 10%, for example, then this would actually represent a growing market, and potentially more profitability. ⓢ Using demographic trends is useful for assessing the market Umbro are in, but Umbro also needs to use other methods of market research such as Mintel reports to avoid the risk of basing decisions on an incomplete picture of the market, thus risking profitability. ⚓ In conclusion, the implications of the above trends on Umbro would depend upon external factors such as the social trend of the growing popularity of football outside of its traditional fan base and whether Umbro can continue to secure lucrative contracts with leading club and national teams. ⓤ

ⓔ **17/20 marks awarded** ⓐ The student gives a definition of demographic trends, gaining 1 mark and Level 1. **b–e** The student explains the demographic trends in the stimulus material in detail, gaining 4 marks and Level 2 (5 marks so far). ⓕ The student gives a negative implication for Umbro of the trends in context but doesn't relate this to the issue of profitability, so gains 1 mark and Level 2 (6 so far). **g,h** The student develops the implication in more detail in context, gaining only 1 more mark and Level 2 (7 marks so far). ⓘ The student gives a negative implication for Umbro's profits in context and gains 1 mark and Level 2 (8 so far). ⓙ A judgement and recommendation are made but as no evaluation has taken place yet it gains no marks. **k–m** The student evaluates the benefit to Umbro of developing products for the 50+ demographic trends in context, gaining 4 marks and Level 3 (12 so far). **n–s** The student evaluates the problem with using demographic trends to make business decisions in context, gaining a further 3 marks and Level 4 (15 so far). ⓣ The student gives a judgement as to the usefulness of demographic trends to Umbro and broadens this to include MOPS to gain 1 mark and AO4 (16 so far). ⓤ The student gives a conclusion in context of the use of demographic trends, also relating it to the wider market, gaining 1 mark and Level 4 (17 marks in total).

Student A gives a reasonably concise answer in context but fails to make sufficient arguments to ensure a reasoned judgement and recommendation regarding the whole of the question. The question effectively misses an evaluation of the 16–25 demographic. However, as the student has provided a balanced and evaluated argument regarding the 50+ demographic in terms of profitability, it still earns a C grade. Student B makes very good use of the data to back up their assessment of demographic trends and their relationship to the two suggested approaches for Umbro. There are clear chains of argument and the student uses the negative aspects of demographics to highlight the potential for profitability with the 50+ option. Both options are evaluated in a sophisticated way, showing wide-ranging and coherent arguments. However, the student fails to make a clear recommendation as to which approach Umbro should take and why – an important aspect of answering this type of question – meaning they cannot achieve full marks. Despite this the student still gains an A grade.

Knowledge check answers

1 Large market of customers, undifferentiated.

2 Allows Lindt to sell in greater volume while still maintaining a perception of a luxury brand and premium pricing.

3 Offering a lower price for a product means demand will rise.

4 Qualitative research could be used to see whether potential customers were happy with the taste and price, and changes made before full market launch.

5 The size of the sample for undertaking primary market research may be too small to draw adequate conclusions about how the product should be developed, priced and marketed.

6 Market mapping's aim is to spot a need or want that is not currently covered by products in the market whereas market segmentation divides a market into smaller sets of customers in order to satisfy those customers' needs.

7 Ford may increase supply of its cars as the robots replacing the workers are new technology, which is likely to make production cheaper. The supply curve for Ford will shift to the right, indicating greater supply.

8 The business, such as Apple, can raise prices with little effect on the demand for its product or service.

9 Bread, fruit, milk, vegetables.

10 a) Boeing: function (speed and safety) plus economic manufacture; b) Gucci: aesthetics and function; c) Barratt Homes: economic manufacture and function.

11 Liverpool football club is sponsored by Subway, Taylor Swift is sponsored by Pepsi and Lewis Hamilton, the Formula One racing driver, is sponsored by Monster energy drinks.

12 Nike's brand is linked to the success of the famous footballer as customers will associate his success with Nike's products and pay a premium to buy them.

13 As Huawei is a new phone manufacturer it does not have the reputation and brand image to be able to sell its phones at the same price as Apple due to initial lack of customer demand. So a lower-priced product may tempt customers to try its new phone.

14 One that has a strong brand image.

15 Apple adopted an extension strategy for the iPhone 5s.

16 Aldi may multi-skill its workforce, such as having employees able to both stack shelves and work on the checkout, in order to ensure wage costs are kept to a minimum, with savings passed on to customers through lower prices.

17 A difference between redundancy and dismissal is that being made redundant means the job no longer exists whereas being dismissed means the job is still available for another employee to take.

18 As there will be more managers to supervise staff making food, the food should be of a higher quality, leading to higher customer satisfaction and ultimately more profit.

19 Employees will be encouraged to work as a team, with managers listening to their ideas and opinions, thus encouraging creative ideas for new products.

20 With every worker benefiting from any increased profits of the business, it is likely to motivate them to be more productive and give higher customer satisfaction, leading to higher sales and profit.

21 As job rotation means employees from different roles do various jobs on the production line, in a new role they are likely to spot working practices that can be done better using processes in other jobs they have done on the production line, thus improving quality overall.

22 With a laissez-faire style the employees are encouraged to make their own decisions within the boundaries set by the leader, but with an autocratic style the employees make no decisions – the leader has sole responsibility for this.

23 Richard Branson has a number of traits associated with being a good entrepreneur, including self-confidence and a vision of how his idea will become a success.

24 An entrepreneur is responsible for all the risks and rewards in the business whereas an intrapreneur may take risks to solve a problem for the business but may not receive all the rewards as a result.

25 By having a clear and well-researched business plan to show the bank that giving them a loan is a good risk as they are highly likely to be able to pay it back.

26 As the products have not been tested on animals and are made from natural plant extracts, many customers feel they are buying products that protect the environment and this encourages customer loyalty and enables The Body Shop to sell products at a premium price.

27 Resilience, as there have been many times in tennis matches when Andy Murray has been losing but has still fought back to become a champion, a characteristic which Under Armour feels will help sell its products.

28 Social and ethical objectives – customers and the countries where BP digs for oil will need to be reassured that the environment and safety of the company's operations are taken seriously, above profit.

29 A sole trader is a business with one owner whereas a partnership has at least two owners.

30 As staff also have a share in the business they have greater motivation to ensure John Lewis meets customer needs, as they will share in the success or failure of the business through potential dividend payments.

31 As the business has spent £500 on advertising it will have forgone an alternative use of these funds, such as paying for staff overtime or offering customers a discount on a product.

Index